Other Books by Marilyn Brown Oden

Fiction

Crested Butte: A Novel

Nonfiction

Published by Upper Room Books

Manger and Mystery:
An Advent Adventure

Through the East Window:
Prayers and Promises for Living with Loss

Wilderness Wanderings:
A Lenten Pilgrimage

Abundance

Joyful Living in Christ

MARILYN BROWN ODEN

UPPER
ROOM BOOKS®
NASHVILLE

ABUNDANCE: Joyful Living in Christ
© 2002 by Marilyn Brown Oden
All rights reserved.

The Upper Room Web site: www.upperroom.org

An extension of the copyright page is found on page 125.

Unless otherwise noted, scripture quotations are from the New Revised Standard Version
of the Bible. Copyright © 1989 by the Division of Christian Education of the National
Council of the Churches of Christ in the United States of America. All rights reserved.

Cover design: Gore Studio
Interior design: Margo Shaw and Nancy J. Cole
First Printing: 2002

Library of Congress Cataloging-in-Publication Data
Oden, Marilyn Brown.
  Abundance : joyful living in Christ / Marilyn Brown Oden.
    p. cm.
Includes bibliographical references.
  ISBN 0-8358-0974-9 (alk. paper)
  1. Christian life—Methodist authors. 2. Christian life—Study and teaching. I. Title.
  BV4501.3 .O34 2002
  248.4—dc21   2002002055

Printed in the United States of America

For
Barbara McCormick
and
Lovers Lane United Methodist Church

Gratitudes

This book is based on my presentations for the James C. and Barbara McCormick Distinguished Speaker Forum at Lovers Lane United Methodist Church in Dallas, Texas. I am grateful for that opportunity, which gave me the discipline to read timely books and to bring order to thoughts that had been rattling around in my mind.

I am grateful for the pastoral leadership of that church and for the congregation, whose mission outreach makes a significant difference not only in the Dallas area but also in the global community. I am grateful that through this lectureship I met Barbara McCormick, a new friend and remarkable person, who told me the story of her late husband, James C. McCormick, a model of courage and leadership.

I am grateful to Bishop Rueben P. Job, who ushers me toward a deeper spirituality and helps me look at life through the lenses of gratitude and abundance.

I am grateful to Bill, Danna Lee, Dirk, Valerie, Bryant, Angela, Chelsea, Sarah, Nathan, and Graham, who entered my life in that order and are my closest partners in the dance of abundance.

—Marilyn Brown Oden

Contents

Wake up, O sleeper,
rise from the dead.

—Ephesians 5:14, NIV

For those who awaken
to life through surprise,
death lies behind,
not ahead.

—Brother David Steindl-Rast
Gratefulness, The Heart of Prayer:
An Approach to Life in Fullness

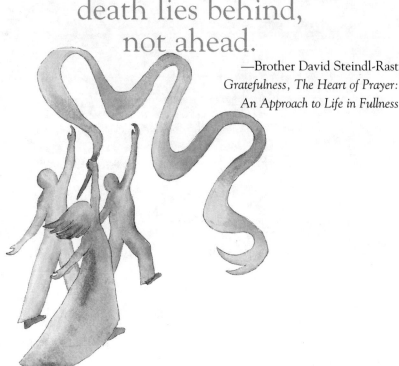

1

Seeking the Secret

Handing out life to those who love me,
filling their arms with life—armloads of life!
—Proverbs 8:21, THE MESSAGE

"Armloads of life!" Living abundantly. What is the secret? Where do we seek it?

Consumerism bombards us with an answer: Abundant life is found in the external. This philosophy distorts abundant living into what we can buy and whom we can best. Just eat this or drink that, wear this or drive that. While driving on the Dallas Tollway, I saw this bumper sticker: YOU ARE WHAT YOU DRIVE.

I don't think so!

"Do not give your heart to that which does not satisfy your heart," warned Abba Poemen in the fifth century. External things satisfy the ego temporarily, but not the heart. In time a feeling of void returns—no matter what we drive!

Jesus offers a different message from consumerism: "I came that they may have life, and have it abundantly" (John 10:10). He didn't proclaim that he came to give his followers abundant wealth, abundant power, or abundant good luck. He came that we might have abundant *life*.

Many (most?) Americans come closer to living chaotically than living abundantly. Sometimes this chaos feels imposed upon us. Think traffic and orange barrels. (And when they build it,

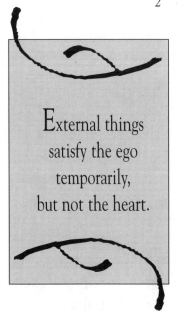

External things
satisfy the ego
temporarily,
but not the heart.

we will come!) More traffic—more orange barrels!

Or junk mail targeted for certain zip codes. Priority! Urgent! Don't miss this! (Why doesn't the postal service just contract directly with a recycling center and leaving us out of the loop?)

Or the phone. When we answer, we're apt to hear a computer instead of a friend. And when we call, we're likely to reach another computer voice: "To better serve you ... punch 1 if . . ." (To *better* serve us?!)

We have a lot to tune out if we are going to tune in to living abundantly.

What is the secret? Where do we seek it?

I gained insight about living abundantly while on retreat with my husband, Bill, at the Taizé Community in France. Brother Roger began the community during World War II to help bring world peace and Christian unity, hoping to make the earth a better place. He dreamed of having a dozen brothers. Today there are more than a hundred, and tens of thousands of people each year from all around the globe retreat to Taizé.

Picture the setting of the Taizé worship service: it happens in a huge, dark barn of a room. An altar filled with a myriad of candles.

Icons shining like gold in the candlelight. Fabrics in flame colors draped behind the altar. The brothers process in two by two, coming down a greenery-bordered aisle into the midst of worshipers, and kneeling in prayer. Jammed around them, filling the room, are more than five thousand people sitting on the floor—most of them youth and young adults—being quiet! Praying. Singing. Hearing the scriptures in many languages. Three times a day. Every day.

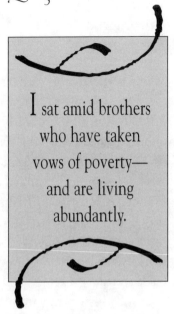

I sat amid brothers who have taken vows of poverty—and are living abundantly.

Brother Roger invited Bill and me to have lunch with the brothers. One of the highest privileges of my life was being seated beside this man of humility, with pure heart and strong character, the gentlest of gentlemen. (It is as close as I will ever get to sitting at the right hand of the Christ!) Lunch is their main meal, a celebration of God's bounty and goodness. We ate outside on this beautiful summer day, all of us together at a long line of tables under a double row of ancient trees. The tree branches arched together above us, and a cloudless blue sky peeked through the leaves. Brother Roger, now in his eighties, welcomed us as guests, reported the world news (obtained from the Internet), and shared what was on his heart. Then we ate in silence with taped classical music playing in the background. I sat amid brothers who have taken vows of poverty—and are living abundantly.

What is the secret? Where do we seek it?

There is no doubt that our external situation can foster or impede living abundantly. But it is not the final factor. Life in abundance is not about being conformed to this world but being transformed by God's healing love. It is rooted in our inner life.

Last summer I walked the labyrinth at Chartres Cathedral in France. A spiritual labyrinth differs from a maze. The labyrinth has no tricks or traps. It is a journey that goes toward the center and, once close to the center, begins going outward again toward the world. It takes us repeatedly toward the center and outward and back to the center again.

Our journey toward abundant living is like walking a spiritual labyrinth repeatedly, from an ever deepening inner space. We walk toward the center to be transformed by God's love; then we walk outward to transform our small space in the world by reflecting God's love. There is no intention to trick us or get us lost along the journey. But there is mystery. Always mystery. And awe. And amazing grace.

What is the secret? Where do we seek it?

Actually, the secret to living abundantly is no secret at all. It is as well-known as the Great Commandment. Indeed, it is the Great Commandment.

I used to think—and I've written—that we love God by loving others. Instead of walking the spiritual labyrinth in an inward/

outward pattern, I ran laps around it, racing frantically from mission to mission. But Jesus didn't say to do that. He said that the first commandment is, "You shall love the Lord your God with all your heart, and with all your soul, and with all your mind, and with all your strength" (Mark 12:30). That means loving God directly—going in toward the center. But it doesn't mean remaining there. For Jesus added: "The second is this, 'You shall love your neighbor as yourself.'

Loving God involves moving in toward the center, but it doesn't mean remaining there.

There is no other commandment greater than these" (Mark 12:31). We show our love for God by going outward again into the world and loving others.

Our journey is ongoing; our transformation is multidimensional. The path of our spiritual labyrinth does not lead to achievement but to awakening, turning us in new directions along the way. Thomas Merton said, "If we could let go of our own obsession with what we *think* is the meaning of it all, we might be able to hear [God's] call and follow [God] in [God's] mysterious, cosmic dance."[1] In this dance we move inward and outward, again and again, to be transformed and to transform; we become more aware of what to embrace, what to enhance, and what to relinquish.

2
Longing for Belonging

Beloved, let us love one another, because love is from God; . . .
Whoever does not love does not know God, for God is love . . .
In this is love, not that we loved God but that he loved us . . .
No one has ever seen God;
if we love one another, God lives in us,
and his love is perfected in us . . .
God is love, and those who abide in love abide in God,
and God abides in them.

—1 John 4:7-16

One dimension of living abundantly is community. As Christians we are to love our neighbor.

All of us begin our life journey with a great disconnection. As newborns we experience being shoved from the womb, having our umbilical cord cut. We are tiny, helpless, and aware of separation. Perhaps from that moment on we sense a longing for belonging.

We is a beautiful word, a connotative word that has the power to call forth joy in the speaker and wistfulness in a lonely listener. How often we hear it:

"*We* play golf (go bowling/quilt/play bridge) every Thursday."

"*We* all go out for brunch after early service."

"*We* always spend New Year's together."

We can also be silent. We wear pins with our organization's logo, share secret handshakes, don sweatshirts to show we're

We long to belong to a place we call home.

football fans. (Until our team gets on a losing streak—fickle fans that we are!)

We long for belonging.

A beautiful and vibrant memorial service celebrated the life of my friend who had been an elementary-school teacher. One of the speakers was a former student—now a pastor.

He told about his own mother's death when he was a little boy, and how after her funeral he was accidentally left all by himself. Each of his relatives thought he'd gone home with someone else:

> There I was in my empty house. Alone. And then I saw her coming toward the door. My teacher! Mrs. Holmes.
> And she took me home!
> She took me home!
> She took me home!

Home! How we long to belong to a place we call home! A place where we feel loved and love others, feel cared for and care for others. A place where we're missed if we don't show up.

Elias Chacour speaks of his childhood home. He was born in the Holy Land, a Melkite Christian whose family's spiritual heritage was firmly rooted in the first century, remaining unbroken even in history's dangerous eras when his ancestors had to meet in secret. As a child he lived on family land that could be traced back to Jesus' time. He played among the ancient olive trees, fig orchards, and mustard plants, and could see the landmarks of the stories that Jesus told. His mother loved a hill near their house, the Mount of Beatitudes, where Jesus spoke to a crowd of Galileans. The sense of Jesus' presence and the assurance that he would listen to personal troubles did not seem at all unusual to little Elias. This land where Jesus walked, this town of Biram, was his home.

Then Zionist soldiers came with their guns—men, says Chacour, "not at all like our Jewish neighbors."[1] The soldiers occupied the homes and then told the people that their village was in serious danger, that they must leave immediately and take nothing with them. The people obeyed and then waited and waited for word to return—but were not allowed to reenter their village. Later, when the state of Israel was established in 1948, the exiles of Biram appealed to the Supreme Court of Israel, and after a long time, they won. But when the people tried to return, the Israeli soldiers wouldn't honor the court decision and drove them away again.

Once more the exiles appealed to the courts, explaining the soldiers' defiance. And once again, after a long while, they won. When the elders approached the soldiers with the second court order, they were told that the soldiers needed time to move out, and they could return on December 25. Christmas Day! They rejoiced. When that holy day arrived, they topped the final hill singing a hymn, looked down on Biram . . . and stopped singing.

The soldiers were still there. Tanks and bulldozers surrounded the town—their weapons aimed toward it! As soon as the soldiers saw the men and women and children appear over the hill, they began firing on the ancient village. The Palestinian Christians from Biram stood dazed, unbelieving. The first shell slammed into their old church. They saw bombs strike their homes and stood helplessly, watching them burn down. When the firing ceased, the bulldozing began, completing the destruction of Biram.

Chacour experienced many wounds at the hands of the Zionist soldiers, including being beaten with sticks as a child. But the deepest wound of all was the need for a home, a sense of place. At age twelve he was selected to attend Saint Joseph's Minor Seminary. The first time he sat in the church there, he finally felt once again the familiar presence of Jesus. He says in *Blood Brothers:* "I sat in this inner silence, swaddled in the feeling that in this place—this church, this very bench—I was home."[2]

We long to feel at home with God. We long to belong to a place that reminds us what our hearts know but our minds forget, a place where we *know* we belong to God. There are moments when we feel this—truly feel it. In those rare and precious times, the bush of our heart begins to burn with the fire of oneness with Creator and creation, and for an instant we experience the *yes!* of connection, a holy connection with all that is.

Belong is a word we use with church. We say, "I belong to . . ." (whatever church). Or we ask another person, "What church do you belong to?" When we move, we lose our sense of home, including our "church home." That is one of the reasons moving is so difficult.

I will confess that I have lied. In the sanctuary. My husband is a clergyman, and I have mourned each time we moved. I knew that eventually I'd feel at home and enjoy the new place also, but it didn't help in the moment. I have customarily joined the church on our first Sunday, and then I've had to turn around and face a congregation filled

We long to feel at home with God.

with strangers. Inwardly, I longed to be back in my old, familiar community of faith with people I knew and loved, where I felt a sense of belonging. I would stand there with tears in my heart and a smile on my face.

Those new good folk—probably missing their old clergy family as much as I was missing our old congregation—also smiled as they came forward to greet and welcome me. At some point the inevitable question would be asked: "Are you glad to be here?"

And then, fearing they wouldn't understand if I responded honestly that I would be glad in time, I stood right there in the sanctuary and lied! "I'm delighted," I said. The word *delighted* became my inner code for de-lighted, unlit, in the dark time of separation. (Technically, that little interpretive twist may have kept me from lying—but I'm not sure God puts much store in technicalities!)

When we move, we lose our sense of home, including our church home.

Inherent in our longing for belonging is a deep desire for purpose and meaning. Henri Nouwen suggests, "People are only ready to commit themselves to each other when they no longer focus on each other but rather focus together on the larger world beyond themselves."[3] I know from personal experience that my marriage is richer and that our relationship is deeper when Bill and I focus not primarily on each other or ourselves but when together we focus on a common mission.

Nouwen's words cause me to wonder if commitment beyond the self is one of the reasons it is so difficult today to decide to get married in the first place and then, once married, to stick with the commitment. We live in a "me" culture that fosters a magnified but limited view of self that fills the entire picture and excludes a broader vision of the world beyond the self. We focus on number one instead of on oneness.

In my observation, Nouwen's words are also true of congregations. The strongest churches I know have good pastors and committed laity who do not focus primarily on themselves but focus together on spiritual growth (to be transformed) and on common missions outside their walls (to transform). A collection of self-centered "me's" does not make a strong "we."

Two experiences in Tallinn, Estonia, demonstrated for me that

Nouwen's words can also be applied to communities. Bill and I were in Estonia right after the failed 1991 coup d'état in the Soviet Union. To keep out Russian tanks, boulders blocked the Old Town gates like stones at the entry to a tomb. On the Old Town square that gray day, downcast individuals stood silently in the rain, waiting to buy bread in their habitual long lines, suspicious and alienated from one another and their society, bent beneath the weight of survival.

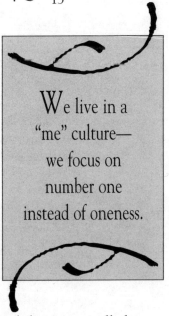

We live in a "me" culture— we focus on number one instead of oneness.

Three years later we returned and found the stones rolled away and a resurrection! The city was alive with renovation and new businesses. The downcast individuals had become a people with vision and hope, united in commitment to a common purpose, and growing in confidence that they could change the world around them. Even the sun was shining.

We long to belong, to know a kind of belonging that gives us purpose and meaning.

The word *synergy*, a term from biology, has been popularized as meaning "the whole is greater than the sum of its parts." That, however, is only half the story. *Synergy* is rooted in the Latin word *synergismus*—"working together"—and is properly defined as "*the*

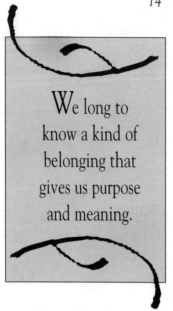

We long to know a kind of belonging that gives us purpose and meaning.

qualities of a whole which are not explainable by a study of its parts."[4] In *The Left Hand of Eden*, William Ashworth reminds us that "the whole may just as well be *less than* the sum of its parts."[5] For me, that terrible Tuesday in September 2001 offers a horrendous example of the latter. Individuals surely became lesser together under the influence of Osama bin Laden than they would have been separately, apart from that influence.

Yet, when we belong to a community that gives us a sense of constructive meaning, positive purpose, and connection to God's creatures in God's world, we find that through caring together we become a synergistic force that is greater than the sum parts of the separate individuals.

The people of Tallinn demonstrated this synergy to me. While there the second time, I spoke at a Methodist women's meeting. A new friend told me the story about how they had ultimately freed themselves from Russian control—without spilling any blood:

> I remember that day so well. The Russian soldiers pointed their guns. We were scared, but drew courage from each other. We stood together. Some ten thousand of us. Arm in arm. Shoulder to shoulder. Making a human chain. We moved forward. Slowly. Bravely, if I may say so. Gradually, we backed the Russians down the hill.

Without touching them.
Without violence.
Without guns.

Together, we moved them out of our city. They were gone! And not a drop of Estonian blood was spilled!

My friend's eyes came back from her memory screen, and she smiled at me. "That's very important to us, you know. There are so few of us Estonians left." What a memory! What a story to pass on from generation to generation!

Bill and I were still there two days later when the ferry named the *Estonia* set out as usual. We had grown accustomed to seeing it anchored outside our hotel window.

Through caring together we become a synergistic force that is greater than the sum parts of separate individuals.

But this time it did not return. It capsized and sank, drowning five hundred Estonians. I attended Tallinn's requiem Mass for the victims, an outsider who also mourned the loss of all those lives.

We long to belong, to feel that we are part of a bit of humanity we can call our own, part of a community that makes us feel greater than ourselves. We long to participate in the wondrous cosmic dance, with its ever changing steps and scenes and its never changing sacredness.

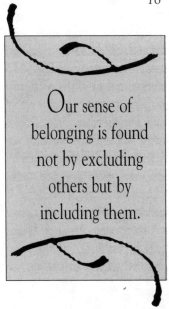

Our sense of belonging is found not by excluding others but by including them.

Once while making the long drive to my mother's home in western Oklahoma, I listened to Charles Kuralt's enjoyable tape about traveling across America. He said, "Society has to do with who is in and who is out." Traditionally, that would be an appropriate definition. But when groups and races of people base their belonging on excluding others, they follow a negative path to self-identity. Exclusivity fosters a false image of other groups, races, and nations. Carried to the extreme, it can evoke conflict and even justify cruelty. Rather than standing shoulder to shoulder, we bump shields.

Our own belonging is found not by excluding others but by including them. When that happens, we experience with Nouwen "the joy of being a part of that vast variety of people—of all ages, colors, and religions—who together form the human family."[6] Jesus said: "Where two or three are gathered in my name, I am there among them" (Matt. 18:20). Three hundred years later, Saint Basil asked pointedly: "Whose feet shall the hermit wash?" Wherever we experience the Christ and his call to community and to servanthood, we experience God's transforming love and begin to taste the meaning of living abundantly.

3
Yearning and Discerning

To one he gave five talents, to another two, to another one,
to each according to his ability . . .
Then the one who had received the one talent
also came forward, saying,
"Master, . . . I was afraid, and I went and hid your talent
in the ground."
—Matthew 25:15, 24a, 25

*D*iscerning our calling is a dimension of living abundantly. Jesus implied a love for self when he said to love your neighbor as yourself. Just as the word *we* is important on this journey, so is the word *I*. In *Confessions*, Augustine said that people "go forth to wonder at the heights of mountains, the huge waves of the sea, the broad flow of the rivers, the extent of the ocean, and courses of the stars, and omit to wonder at themselves."[1]

Before our grandson had surgery last summer, our daughter and I took him to Disneyland. All the characters were there for photo ops: Pluto, Piglet, and Pooh, to name a few. Different performers became those characters at different times of the day. It didn't matter who. Appearance was all that counted—costume, mask, and gestures.

You and I are not Pluto, Piglet, or Pooh. But could someone else play me? Play you? Just climb into your life and zip up the costume, don the mask, master your gestures and speech patterns—

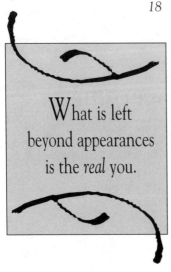

What is left beyond appearances is the *real* you.

like a Disneyland Pooh. Would that be you? Of course not! What is left beyond appearances is the *real* you. All that inner stuff that cannot be duplicated.

In the book *Corelli's Mandolin*, by Louis de Bernieres, Pelagia says of her father: "I thought then for the first time how small and frail he was, how beaten and betrayed, and I realized that without his soul he was so light and thin that even I could lift him." It is our soul, this inner part—unique, unrepeatable, unexchangeable, and irreplaceable—that can be transformed by God's healing love, even when we are beaten and betrayed.

Do you ever feel like a character in someone else's life story?

Perhaps a son performing in a father's play?

Or a wife dancing on a husband's stage?

Or a parent living through a child—of whatever age?

Or playing out someone's script written for you in childhood?

Or exchanging that script for one written by a social group or corporation?

Perhaps we focus on image—maybe even hiring an image consultant. The problem with changing our image is that our hearts aren't involved. Changing our appearance may increase bids for us on the auction block, but it doesn't help us discover who we are essentially, authentically, core deep. The capacity for living abundantly isn't about packaging; it has to do with what remains when the tinsel ties are tossed and the wrapping paper comes off. For the Christian, "image" relates to the image of God in each of us. Now that's an image worth pursuing!

For the Christian, "image" relates to the image of God in each of us.

Whatever the source, we spend precious time of our limited life span inhabiting an unlived-in life. In *Let Your Life Speak*, Parker Palmer comments, "The life I am living is not the same as the life that wants to live in me."[2]

It isn't uncommon for a bishop's spouse to feel like a character in another's life story. I've had wonderful experiences as the wife of a bishop, and I'm grateful for all the opportunities. Yet, sometimes I feel a division between me and my role as bishop's wife. Frequently when I'm on "the bishop's turf"—which is much of the time—I tend to fade away. I choose to stand silently beside him. Or slightly behind him. A smiling shadow, hiding behind image. Bill certainly doesn't do this to me. I do it to myself. (Bishops' spouses develop a propensity for appearing invisible!)

Recently I spent a few days at a Benedictine monastery to glue my fragmented soul back together. I had made the arrangements and used my name—no bishop attached. But the good fathers and brothers at the monastery remembered "the tall bishop" who used to take his cabinet there for retreats when Bill was bishop in Louisiana. (And Catholics hold bishops in high regard.)

The Benedictines welcomed me as a precious child of God, for they welcome everyone as the Christ. Those three days at Saint Joseph Abbey—with the rhythm of worship, silence, sense of holiness, and the gift of community—were indescribably meaningful to me.

On my last day I was taking a walk and passed a monk sitting on a bench under a live oak tree that dripped with Spanish moss. He introduced himself and said, "You leave today."

"Yes. It has been wonderful to be here."

"Your husband is a bishop." His eyes twinkled. "We've been watching you."

I smiled. "Bishops' wives are a bit of a rarity in your faith." We both laughed.

Then with kind face and melodic voice, he said five words I will never forget: "Your presence has blessed us."

Somehow in that moment, a lot of longtime, jumbled perceptions fell into place like those set-aside pieces in a jigsaw puzzle that finally fit a space. I felt as though he took *me* and the *bishop's wife* and merged the two into one. For it was my presence that blessed them, but my presence was more meaningful to them because I am a bishop's wife. Of course! I am both! How could I have been such a slow learner? God's gifts come at the most surprising times from the most amazing places—like this wondrous gift of self-integration that came through a Catholic Benedictine monk.

We are the sum total of all our roles, relationships, and responsibilities. Jesus invites us to be whole persons, this One who came to us without an image consultant and showed us the image of God. We may choose to perform in another's play, dance on another's stage, postpone our deep desires for the benefit of another, or even agree temporarily to act out a script written for us by someone else. But when we make this choice consciously from our deepest part, the result is a gift out of the fullness of life—not something stolen away, leaving us empty.

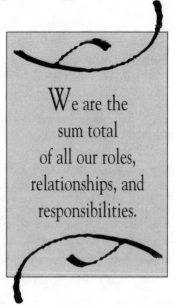

We are the sum total of all our roles, relationships, and responsibilities.

Joan Chittister of the Order of Saint Benedict says: "To have something to give another, we have to have something of substance in ourselves."[3] To a large degree, that "substance" results from our choices. What we do from day to day and the overall pattern we establish is, for the most part, the sum of our choices, made intentionally or by default. The choices that bring feelings of being close to God—whatever those choices may be for each of us—are faithful, full of faith. In doing them, we lean toward abundant life. On the other hand, the choices that bring feelings of being distant from God—again, whatever those choices may be for each of us—

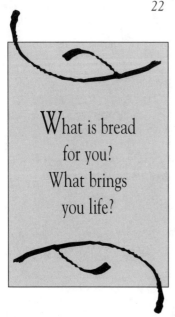

What is bread
for you?
What brings
you life?

are unfaithful, not full of faith. They block abundant life. "People ruin their lives by their own stupidity, so why does GOD always get blamed?" (Proverbs 19:3, THE MESSAGE). The answer may be that it is far easier for us to place blame than to face change.

The little book *Sleeping with Bread* tells a story about children in bombing raids during World War II. Left orphaned and starving, they were rescued and placed in refugee camps. Many of these children couldn't sleep at night. They feared waking up and being once again homeless and hungry. Someone thought of "giving each child a piece of bread to hold at bedtime. With that bit of bread in their little hands," these children could finally sleep in peace. All through the night the bread reminded them, "'Today I ate, and I will eat again tomorrow.'"4

What is bread for you? What brings you life—what do you miss and regret when you allow it to be buried by other demands? What is that special thing that, if absent, leaves you feeling hungry, perhaps homeless, maybe even hopeless? This bread, whatever it is for each of us, is our calling—our specific God-given gift, our deep purpose.

In "God and Business," an article in *Fortune*, Mark Gunther tells about Jose Zeilstra, a Christian whose lay calling has led her into the business world. A prominent management consultant, she lets the Bible guide her as much as corporate policies and business texts. She lives her faith by encouraging business executives to "err a little bit on the generous side" and to "focus on people and values." She argues for what's right and tries to act with compassion. Though she avoids the "G" word (God) at work, she says, "Ultimately I'm working for God. There is no higher calling than to serve God, and that does

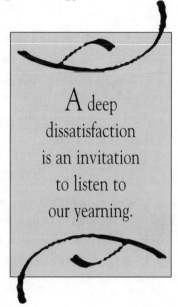

A deep dissatisfaction is an invitation to listen to our yearning.

not mean only within the church. Ultimately, your life, whether it's work, family, or friends, is part of a larger plan."[5]

Sometimes a sense of dissatisfaction whispers to us from deep within. We feel a stirring, a yearning. If you know what I'm talking about, don't stuff this yearning down without a hearing. Don't be afraid of it. Chittister reminds us, "Trust your dissatisfactions."[6] A deep dissatisfaction is an invitation to listen to our yearning. To reflect on our sense of emptiness. To pray. To try to discern its source and its message. For it is our own calling that invites us to respond, our own life that we are intended to live.

One afternoon I was talking with a woman in her late thirties who was facing a divorce. Her difficult marriage had resulted in a detour from the path she yearned to take. She spoke softly: "The tears come sometimes. For the things that weren't, and now can't ever be . . . Do you know what I mean?"

Don't we all!

I am reminded again of Pelagia in *Corelli's Mandolin*. The old woman says, "O my poor life that never was." We mourn those dreams denied—those things that happened that we can't undo. And those things that didn't happen—and now can never be.

The good news is that we don't have to remain stuck. Each new sunrise offers us an opportunity to begin again from wherever we are—so that when tomorrow's tomorrow comes, we don't look back and mourn *this* today.

There is another bit of good news. Sometimes we give up too soon. Sometimes a dream that appears denied is merely delayed. When I wrote *Through the East Window*, a book that deals with nine kinds of loss, I included the shattered dream. As an example, I cited the denial of my dream of a novel, *Crested Butte*, completed but unpublished and sitting on the closet shelf gathering dust. I wrote about how part of me still dreams of writing fiction, and how "every once in a while Vini calls to me in the night." When I wrote those words, Vini (the main character) woke up! And I was not released until I pulled the manuscript down from the shelf, dusted it off, and began to revise it once more. Since I hadn't worked on my novel in a long while, I came at it from a different perspective, a deeper place. Finally, I knew that it was as good as I could make it, and that brought a sense of satisfaction. I even found myself glad that it hadn't been published earlier when it was less than it could be. At long last, instead of suffocating on a closet shelf, Vini breathes in a book! I am shamelessly joyful about the dream I once thought denied but instead was merely delayed until the fullness of time.

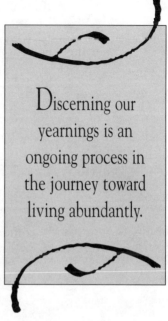

Discerning our yearnings is an ongoing process in the journey toward living abundantly.

Discerning our yearnings is an ongoing process in the journey toward living abundantly, a process filled with surprise. Thomas Merton says, "We are invited to forget ourselves on purpose, cast our awful solemnity to the winds and join in the . . . dance."[7] Our part in the dance is to become aware of our gifts and to be a conduit, giving our gifts to others in praise of God. And never giving up. Pelagia also said, "I feel like an unfinished poem." *Yes!* We are all unfinished poems. We always will be. Beautiful, open-ended, unfinished poems.

4
Healing Our Hearts

Keep vigilant watch over your heart;
that's where life starts.

—Proverbs 4:23, THE MESSAGE

So, community and calling. Is that all?

No. There is more. We need healing for our hearts—our wounded and broken hearts. Jesus said to love God with all our hearts. In the Hebrew scriptures, heart represents the total person. It is the center of emotions, discernment, devotion, and wisdom. Healing the heart regenerates the whole self. We begin with confession.

Secrets make us sick, especially secrets of the heart. Isaiah says: "He feeds on ashes, a deluded heart misleads him" (Isa. 44:20a, NIV).

Do you have a secret side? a shadow side? a side you want to hide—even from yourself? Perhaps especially from yourself? Does it sneak out now and then and take over?

Probably. (Unless I'm the only one in need of confession.) Our shadow side is part of us. A young and immature part, perhaps a

Secrets make us sick.

damaged part, perhaps a scared part—but nonetheless, a part of us.

The theologian Evagrius (born in 345 C.E.) classified eight categories of human frailty. He didn't call them sins. He was not interested in evoking judgment but in healing hearts. That was almost seventeen hundred years ago. Could Evagrius's categories still be relevant today? Look at the following list and see what you think:

1. *Sorrow.* Do people still fall into sorrow and despair?

2. *Gluttony.* Do we still habitually overeat?

Our attitude toward food provides an interesting clue to our affluence on the global continuum. When sitting down at the dinner table, some of us note mentally whether there is enough food. Or, taking for granted that there is always enough, some of us note whether the food tastes good. Or, accustomed to delicious plenty, some of us note whether the food is well presented. (Hmmm.)

Food is not our only means of gluttony. Gluttony can also pertain to our other habits of overindulgence.

3. *Lust.* Is lust still part of the shadow side, in our hearts if not in our habits?

4. *Vainglory.* Does vanity still take control, and we find ourselves dependent on praise or recognition?

5. *Acedia.* Do we still fall into sloth? boredom? a sense of purposelessness?

Apathy

6. *Pride*. Does excessive pride still creep out, unleashing arrogance and a need to control? Proverbs 15:33 reminds us: "First you learn humility, then you experience glory" (THE MESSAGE).

7. *Avarice*. Does greed still reside in the shadow side? The ancient Isidore warned that greed is insatiable, for people afflicted with it always feel a need for something else, and the more they have, the more they want. In all these centuries that hasn't changed.

Greed happens when God gives us manna, and we wail for a banquet.

Some of us are greedy for money, power, prestige—for honors, compliments, center stage. Or we crave information, things, clothes. Greed happens when God gives us manna, and we wail for a banquet. Or when our plate of opportunities is heaped high, and we vie for seconds. Greed uses others—and then tosses them away, shriveled. It eclipses the common good.

Healing our hearts of greed calls us to get down on our knees and pray for God to forgive our ingratitude, and then it calls us to rise and practice generosity. Recently I was in Colorado with my daughter and grandson. During worship, he put his two dimes in the offering plate, and I was elated. His allowance is two dollars a week, and he is being taught to give 10 percent—as his mother was taught.

But then I saw her put in her tithing check, and I wanted to say, "No, no, no! Not you, child. You are a single mom with a

Healing our hearts
of grudges
and anger
calls us to our knees.

teacher's salary and a son who has had seven surgeries within six years. Not you!"

Ohhh! How often we find excuses to be excused—or to excuse our children—from generosity!

8. *Anger.* Does anger still take control?

Feeling angry is not the major issue; doing harm is the major issue. We can damage ourselves through habitual simmering or the internal impact of a fit of rage. We can also hurt another person. When we allow our anger to harm another—even if our anger is justified—we turn away from God. Ignatius of Antioch, who lived in the first century, warned that God does not dwell where divisions and bad feelings exist. Every time we pray the Lord's Prayer, we link our own forgiveness to our forgiving-ness.

Anger can weigh us down with the grudges we carry. We keep them locked safely in the deposit box of our souls, savoring them and avoiding reconciliation. Our grudges give us an excuse to arm ourselves for combat, to venture forth expecting and perpetuating conflict. On guard against a begrudged person or group, our responses range from cool suspicion to heated aggression, which evoke a similar response in the other. And neighbors end up not speaking; congregations end up polarized; nations end up at war.

Healing our hearts of grudges and anger calls us again to our knees, this time to pray for the one who has harmed us. And this doesn't mean praying for revenge! It means praying sincerely for the harmer's well-being. This is so *hard*. But with continued prayer, we experience a mystery. In time something changes within us. In time our grudge fades, our anger subsides. In time that person's power over our spirit is disarmed. The one who has harmed us may or may not change. It doesn't matter, for through prayer, God brings healing to our own hearts.

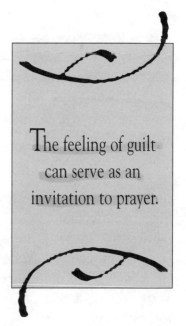

The feeling of guilt can serve as an invitation to prayer.

When we have a problem and our shadow side sneaks out and takes control, we end up with three problems instead of one: We still have the original problem, plus the wake caused by the shadow side, as well as the resulting guilt that can weigh us down.

A notable landscape feature of the Oklahoma panhandle is the way trees bend downward rather than reaching upward. Strong winds have bowed the branches. Those trees remind me of how our guilt burdens bow us. We trudge along with downcast eyes, stooped as though looking for land mines. Our guilt is understandable. Again and again we fall short. But we have a choice—we can lift our eyes to God. When we feel guilty, we can always pray.

Kübler ~
Ross
quote

Brother Roger of the Taizé community says that "the Holy Spirit is light within us," that it "illuminates the shadows of our soul" and "penetrates our inner nights, suffusing them with [God's] invisible presence."[1] One night I lay awake, staring up at the darkness through the skylight above the bed. The skylight framed swirling clouds backlit by moonlight. The clouds whirled at the whim of the wind; the gaps between them narrowed, lengthening like slits; and gradually they overlapped. But they weren't forced into a mold, into some pattern foretold. The breath of the wind blew free, dynamic, unfettered by structure. I watched the clouds witness to the way of the wind, the Spirit wind. But as I continued to look through the skylight, suddenly my eyes tricked me. I saw the clouds stand motionless, framed like the still point of the universe. Yet I was the one moving, caught in the dynamics of the Spirit. I could feel the Spirit's power, its sustaining strength. The night became suffused with God's invisible presence.

The shadow side is not something "out there" but a part of our being. These shadows are not to be feared but entrusted to the winds of the Spirit and disarmed by the invisible light of God's presence. Said T. S. Eliot: "So the darkness shall be the light, and the stillness the dancing."[2]

Our progress toward deep change is slow. Healing our hearts is not a climb mastered by our will. In speaking of the deluded heart, Isaiah goes on to say: "He cannot save himself" (Isa. 44:20). Healing our hearts is more like the rhythm of the tides, an ebb and flow. Breakers come and tidal waves, and our sand castles are washed into the sea. We progress and regress. We grow weary. My German friend Marcus uses the phrase "tired in my heart" to describe that feeling. The journey toward wholeness/holiness is life-long, offered one sunrise at a time.

A spiritual guide can help as we dance across the quicksand of healing our hearts. The person we select to usher us toward spiritual growth needs to be well down the path toward spiritual maturity, to have integrity, to be nonjudgmental and encouraging, to know how to listen, *Accountability* and unafraid to speak the truth in love. If we take spiritual formation seriously, the decision of selecting a spiritual guide ranks right up there with the most important decisions in our lives, for it reshapes our very being.

> A spiritual guide can help as we dance across the quicksand of healing our hearts.

John Wesley taught that holiness is not an outward thing consisting chiefly in two points: "the doing no harm" and "the doing good." He saw holiness as "an inward thing, namely, the life of God in the soul of [humans]; a participation of the divine nature; the mind that was in Christ; or, the renewal of our heart, after the image of [God] that created us."[3]

While driving through a small town one day, I noticed a little church, newly built. A beautiful steeple was included—but it stood on the ground beside the church. How often in our own lives we

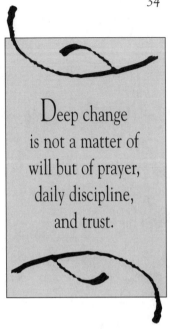

Deep change
is not a matter of
will but of prayer,
daily discipline,
and trust.

leave the steeple on the ground! That way, we can keep it nearby but irrelevant to our inner life.

In writing about Wesleyan spirituality, Bishop Rueben Job reminds us of "the grace to be more than we are" and affirms that God's work of transformation within us "is offered to everyone."[4] Deep change is not a matter of will but of prayer, daily discipline, and trust in God's presence and grace. It requires patience with ourselves. To think that a mere decision will result in permanent change and alleviate all future stumbles is a self-defeating fantasy. An initial step away from merely repeating our past history is to give ourselves to the Mystery. For in so doing, we can begin to focus on living out our lives under the steeple, instead of beside it. We realize with Merton that "no despair of ours can alter the reality of things, or stain the joy of the cosmic dance which is always there. Indeed, we are in the midst of it, and it is in the midst of us, for it beats in our very blood, whether we want it to or not."[5]

I've heard about a heart surgeon, a man of faith, who never begins his task of healing the heart without praying with the patient and the family. Prayer is the first and ongoing step in healing our haunted hearts. It is a safe place to confess our shadow side, to reflect and repent, to experience redemption and grace, and to begin anew. John Climacus, a seventh-century Mount Sinai monk, described prayer as "an illumination of the mind" and said, "Through prayer we find peace for our souls and healing for our wounds."

Through prayer
we find peace
for our souls
and healing
for our wounds.
—JOHN CLIMACUS

If secrets make us sick, then part of the "wellness program" is daring to pull our shadow side out into the light of God's unconditional love. We set before God this young, scared, defensive, broken part of us. And God wraps it tenderly in a quilt of loving forgiveness and rocks it gently, quietly singing a lullaby of healing.

5
Reviewing Our Worldview

Do not be conformed to this world,
but be transformed by the renewing of your minds,
so that you may discern what is the will of God—
what is good and acceptable and perfect.

—Romans 12:2

So, community, calling, and confession. Is that all?

No. There is still more. We have the capacity to choose our mind-set. Jesus said to love God not only with all our hearts and all our souls, but also with all our minds. Living abundantly is less about possessions than perceptions. It relates more to attitude than accumulation. It is a way of thinking, a way of interpreting the events that affect our lives and of interpreting the words and actions of people. To a large degree, how we view the world is a matter of choice.

Let's compare two mind-sets: scarcity versus abundance. Henri Nouwen, Parker Palmer, and Walter Brueggemann all have written about this topic.[1] Also I dealt briefly with it in *Manger and Mystery*. I want to pursue it further because I am convinced that we underestimate the power of the scarcity-abundance dichotomy and its impact on how we live.

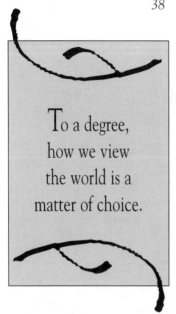

To a degree, how we view the world is a matter of choice.

An abundance worldview is at the opposite end of a continuum from a scarcity worldview. Each view offers contrary vantage points and perspectives that result in different basic perceptions of God and humanity. Either can become the north of our inner compass, giving us direction.

A mind-set of scarcity breeds scarcity. It is based on fear and it promotes fear. It views God's world as sparse and dangerous. Boundaries draw in, and the scope of possibilities narrow. The scarcity syndrome fosters fear of losing face or place. It sucks us down into the quicksand of suspicion, and we tend to guard what is ours and take more than is necessary from others and the earth. Things hoarded and hidden eventually rot or rust, become faded or forgotten. Even unshared talents shrivel. A scarcity mentality is disabling, for the world and life and relationships are viewed through bars that protect but also imprison.

In contrast, a mind-set of abundance fosters generosity and a shared sense of community, which in turn foster abundant living. The world is the same, but it is viewed as bountiful instead of barren. The horizon stretches out like the big sky of Texas, and possibilities seem unlimited. The abundance syndrome fosters a basic sense of trust. It overcomes suspicion as, through acts of sharing both tangibles and intangibles, we discover that there is enough to go around —enough power and prestige, enough honor and respect, enough love and compassion, enough "loaves and fishes." There is more than enough, for we discover that whatever we give multiplies as it ripples through others' lives. An abundance mentality is enabling, for the world and life and our relationships are viewed through God's grace—God's abundant, amazing grace.

> An abundance mentality is enabling— the world, life, and our relationships are viewed through God's grace.

A scarcity mind-set approaches life with squint-eyed suspicion; an abundance mind-set, with wide-eyed anticipation. Scarcity reaches out with a clutched fist; abundance, with an open hand. Scarcity responds because of duty; abundance, because of delight. Scarcity builds an outer fort; abundance, an inner sanctuary. A scarcity mind-set hardens the heart; an abundance mind-set softens the soul.

It is unlikely, of course, that anyone stands totally at one end or the other of the scarcity-abundance continuum. We fluctuate between the two. Where we land from time to time is influenced somewhat by our current situation and the person or group we are with at the moment. Our position on the continuum also depends, more centrally, on our openness and how often we provide ourselves an opportunity for daily solitude, reflection, and centering.

It is important to understand that we can have physical or economic advantages or a privileged background and retain a mind-set of scarcity; likewise, we can experience physical or economic deprivation or an underprivileged background and still choose an abundance mind-set. A couple of people come to mind: One is blind; the other has one leg. Both are skiers! In each of those situations, a scarcity worldview would be understandable. But it is not inevitable.

James McCormick, a Dallas businessman who started the Kindness Foundation, also comes to mind. As a young man he was struck with polio; at the same time his wife was expecting a baby. He endured the aftermath of the disease for the rest of his life. He knew how it was to live with pain and physical difficulties, including needing to use a wheelchair. But instead of perceiving his future as ruined by these challenges, he courageously chose to make a profound difference in his church and community. Even in his later years, after suffering two heart attacks and cancer, he continued to make that choice. He is no longer alive, but his influence lives on. People like Jim McCormick show us that one whose body is physically challenged can still challenge the rest of us to keep up!

I also think of Frank McCourt, the author of *Angela's Ashes* and *'Tis*. He makes no pretense about his boyhood. He grew up in Ireland in extreme poverty. His father repeatedly disappointed him. But when he looks back over those days, instead of perceiving his hardships to have ruined his life, he views his childhood as happy. A high standard of life does not require a high standard of living.

I recall a story that Brother Patrick at Harmony Hill tells about a bag lady in downtown Little Rock. A monk saw her pushing her full cart at the end of the day, and then she stopped and looked up at the sky. When he tried to talk with her, she ignored him and continued staring toward the western sky. He too looked up, and he saw the sunset's performance, its bright reds and oranges setting the soft bank of clouds afire in the deepening blue sky. Soon it dipped out of sight, and she patted his arm. He looked into her beautiful face and saw her sparkling eyes, the fresh tears on her dirty cheeks, and her radiant, toothless smile. "God," she whispered, "is just too good to me!"[2]

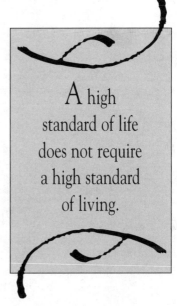

A high standard of life does not require a high standard of living.

Long ago I read *From Death-Camp to Existentialism* by Viktor Frankl, a psychotherapist who survived Auschwitz. One sentence he wrote has stayed with me all these years and has guided me in difficult times: "Everything can be taken from [a person] but one thing: the last of the human freedoms—to choose one's attitude in any given set of circumstances, to choose one's own way."[3] We have habitual thought patterns and reactions and actions. Our interpretations of relationships and life events grow out of these patterns. And these patterns are influenced—if not shaped—by attitude. Since we can choose our attitudes, we have an ultimate choice about changing our habitual ways of thinking, of reacting, and of acting. An abundance mind-set is, to a large degree, a spiritual attitude that can be learned.

This does not mean that the learning process is smooth, easy, and instant. It is just that—a process—and a process requires patience. There is an ancient story about a seeker who went to see a holy man:

"Wise One, how did you become holy?"
"Two words," said the old man.
"Pray tell me, what are they?"
"Right choices."
"But how do I learn to choose correctly?"
"One word."
"Please, Wise One, may I know it?"
"Growth."
"But how do I grow?"
"Two words."
"O, Wise One, please tell me. What are those words?"
"Wrong choices."

Inherent in our wrong choices is the opportunity to grow, rather than to be defeated—which in itself is another choice.

Choosing an abundance mind-set is not easy in our culture. For one thing, there is evil in the world. There is hunger. There is an imbalance of resources. And there is fear, which fosters a scarcity mind-set. Nouwen says, "We are fearful people . . . This fear takes away our freedom and gives our society the power to manipulate us with threats and promises."4

Fear affects our trust level. We were forced to take our first breath in life, but we chose to take our first step. At that point all of us who were physically able had enough trust to risk standing up and moving forward. Time and again. Even after repeated falls. And finally we got it! But somewhere along the way many of us stopped trusting ourselves, or others, or both. And trust in God either never developed or got lost on the journey. We need trust if we are to peek out with one eye from behind scarcity's blinders and risk exposing ourselves to the unfamiliar.

now We fear for the future. We fret and stew over the *What if?*s instead of celebrating the *Wow!*s of God's gifts. Brueggemann tells a story of a mother worried about whether her little boy could get into the right kindergarten.[5] Because if not, then what if he couldn't get into the right prep school? Because if not, then what if he couldn't get into the right college? And if not, then what if he couldn't be connected to the right bank?

The child was only four years old, and his life script was already written! (For some children the same pressure occurs with sports.) The mother in this story meant well, of course. All of us are vulnerable where our children are concerned. But nonetheless, she was fearfully handing him her script for his life rather than allowing him

> Somewhere along the way many of us stopped trusting ourselves, or others, or both. And trust in God got lost on the journey.

the soulful privilege of gently unfolding as a character in his own life story and celebrating the surprising *Wow!*s of his journey into the future.

Choosing an abundance mind-set is difficult, not only because of mistrust and fear for the future but also because the scarcity world-view permeates our culture. Scarcity sells, and the marketing industry knows it.

A scarcity mentality is susceptible to the threat of shortages—so we buy more than we need. Remember Y2K? What a news media filler! What a marketing ploy!

A scarcity mentality is also susceptible to the threat of not getting our share of the world's goodies even in times of plenty—so we buy what our neighbor has. Think of all the entitlement/you-deserve-it commercials. Brueggemann talks about the "Nike Story," which tells us, "Whoever has the most shoes when he dies wins."[6] Do we really believe that?

The scarcity syndrome produces fear of others, and that fear sells all kinds of things—guns, security devices, residences in "safe" neighborhoods, and a wide variety of insurance. Recall this week's news—any week's news. It reinforces fear. Though a small percentage of people commit violent acts, violence makes up a high percentage of news reports, assaulting our ears with the warning wail of a world gone awry. I recall a discussion about how often "news" reporters are willing to sacrifice objectivity and ethics for sensationalism. "Well," a man noted with a shrug, "that's what sells." Salability supposedly absolves responsibility. Do we really believe that?

The dry creekbed of the scarcity syndrome leaves us with a feeling that we're missing something, for we thirst for Life. The creative but sometimes amoral marketing industry bombards the airwaves with thirst quenchers: "This address (or beautifier or cruise or whatever) will give you life!" Do we *really* believe that?

The evangelists of the gospel of consumerism preach suspicion, pessimism, and greed, "these three." Words of scarcity. But it is the New Testament words of abundance—

Consumerism may be the fastest-growing religion in our country.

"faith, hope, and love abide, these three"—that fill the dry creekbed and the inner void that thirsts for more.

Consumerism may be the fastest-growing religion in our country. Brueggemann says that we read the Bible's message occasionally, but we "watch Nike ads every day."[7] Almost unconsciously we buy into the consumerism cult.

Even the church gets caught up in it, tilting The Story toward what is most marketable rather than what is most faithful. An oft-repeated perspective of the church marketing mentality is that if you want your church to grow, it is essential that you . . . guess what? Have an adequate parking lot! (I find it refreshing that one of the largest churches in United Methodism, with more than

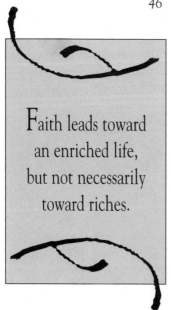

Faith leads toward an enriched life, but not necessarily toward riches.

thirteen thousand members, has a parking lot with seventeen spaces.) Do we really believe that parking our cars conveniently is related to deepening our faith?

Marketing techniques can be helpful to the church if we work toward a vision of the market for The Message instead of a revision of The Message for the market. We've all heard preachers in person or on radio and television who translate the gospel of abundance into the gospel of prosperity, confusing the journey of faith with a path to possessions. And perhaps that even works at times, for we tend to reap what we sow—excluding those zaps beyond our control. How that message appeals to us! It offers us a deal we can't refuse, a good-luck charm or a shortcut on the spiritual labyrinth. But when Jesus talked about having life and having it abundantly, he was not talking about prosperity. Faith in the God of abundance leads toward an enriched life but not necessarily toward riches.

The good news about consumerism is that some business leaders are rethinking materialism that comes at the expense of meaning. In his article "God and Business," Marc Gunther tells about the comment of an executive participating in a conference on work and spirituality: "You get to the top of the ladder and find that maybe it's leaning against the wrong building."[8] Gunther goes on to say that though religion is the last taboo in the business world, some Christians argue that faith works and that eventually spirituality will be welcomed in the business setting for pragmatic reasons. They claim that "the core principles of spirituality—the belief that all individuals have dignity, that we are all interconnected, and that a transcendent being or force defines purpose in human affairs—dovetail with contemporary management thinking about what drives great companies."9 The reason might be questionable, but choosing the fork of

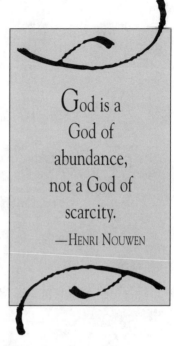

God is a God of abundance, not a God of scarcity.

—HENRI NOUWEN

meaning instead of the fork of materialism seems to be a step on the right path.

Nouwen reminds us in *Bread for the Journey:* "God is a God of abundance, not a God of scarcity."10 But how difficult it is for us to embrace this! We believe in our Creator's unconditional love and grace; yet, we know we don't deserve it—God help our unbelief! We cannot comprehend the God of abundance—this omniscient/transcendent, all-encompassing/personal, unfathomable/close God. It isn't logical. It's a mystery and therefore a matter for the heart.

"The path to God starts at the gates of perception," says Brother David Steindl-Rast.11 A scarcity mentality influences our view of God, and in turn our view of God can reinforce a scarcity

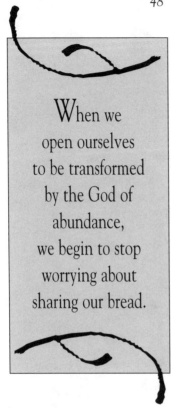

When we
open ourselves
to be transformed
by the God of
abundance,
we begin to stop
worrying about
sharing our bread.

mentality. Through this mentality, SCARCITY we tend to perceive God as one to fear, a punitive God who speaks the word of judgment much louder than grace. Perhaps our doubt that God forgives us makes forgiving others more difficult for us. A scarcity view of God fosters fear, reward motivation, and tit-for-tat. This worldview is burdensome. Through an abundance mentality, we tend to perceive God as the giver of grace, who speaks the language of unconditional love. Perhaps our assurance that God forgives us makes it easier to forgive others. Faith in the God of abundance fosters gratitude.

Brother David also says, "Gratefulness is the measure of our aliveness."[12] While driving through a stretch of road repairs, I came to a sharp curve that veered around a very old and tiny cemetery. At its edge, right in front of me, loomed a big orange sign with black letters: DETOUR. (Gladly! We'll put off the cemetery as long as possible!) Yet, it is an apt warning. If Brother David is right and our aliveness is measured by our gratitude, we may already be sleeping in the cemetery! "Wake up, O sleeper," beckons Ephesians, "rise from the dead" (5:14, NIV). Awake to gratitude!

Jesus asked: "Why are you talking about having no bread? Do you still not perceive or understand? Are your hearts hardened? Do you have eyes, and fail to see? Do you have ears, and fail to hear? And do you not remember?" (Mark 8:17-18).

When we risk reviewing our worldview, opening ourselves to be transformed by the God of abundance, we begin to stop worrying about sharing our bread. We begin to perceive that all is sacred. We begin to understand that the Mystery is beyond our understanding. We begin to soften our hardened hearts. We become grateful for our eyes that see God's multitudinous simple gifts. We become grateful for our ears that hear the song of the Spirit. We remember the One who came to us in a manger and showed us the mystery of God.

We recognize our partner in the dance, and trust is reborn in the space vacated by fear. Brother David suggests that "genuine faith is courageous trust in God's trustworthiness."[13] *Yes!* This trustworthy God of abundance is the One we find on the spiritual labyrinth that leads to living abundantly.

6
Seeing with Our Souls

The Spirit has given each of us
a special way of serving others.

—1 Corinthians 12:7, CEV

Healing our hearts and reviewing our worldview lead to seeing with our souls. We are to love God not only with all our hearts and minds but also with all our souls. Whereas healing our hearts is about waking up, seeing with our souls is about getting up. It has to do with compassion.

When we see with our souls, we become more aware of God's *PAY* *Attention* daily presence. We discover that we do not have to seek the cosmic dance. It comes to us through the simple gifts God offers us: the morning silence before words and works begin. The songs of birds greeting the dawn. The child who tugs on our sleeve and invites us, "Come see." The full orange moon shining through the trees. We look through the eyes of Psalm 103—"God touches all in the heavens and on earth. Everything is full of sacred presence." We begin to realize that anything that happens to us—*anything*—can become a means to spiritual growth. We glimpse what Joan Chittister is talking about when she says, "Everything I do today carries within it a flash of the divine."[1]

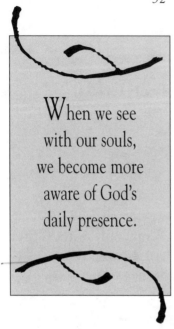

When we see with our souls, we become more aware of God's daily presence.

I attended a Bible study led by Evelyn Laycock. She told an ancient story:

A seeker asked a Wise One: "When will the dawn come? Will it come when I can tell a sheep from a dog?"

"No," said the Wise One. "It will not come when you can tell a sheep from a dog."

"Will it come when I can tell the difference between two kinds of trees?"

"No," said the Wise One. "It will not come when you can tell the difference between two kinds of trees."

"Then when will the dawn come?"

The Wise One answered, "The dawn will come when you can see each person as your sister or your brother."

To see with our souls is to greet the dawn. It is to meet our brothers and sisters where they are and to treat them as though they are already what they can be. The old habitual question "How do I feel when I'm with you?" is exchanged for a new one—"How do you feel when you're with me?" We listen and respond to the other as we would to the Christ.

But how many others? Our brothers and sisters extend around the world. Who is to be in our immediate circle of care? Like the Benedictines, anyone who comes to our door? Everyone we see? What about people in the workplace and grocery store? On the tollway? Caring for others is not something on a to-do list, prescribing a certain number of people and associated with duty. It relates to a natural response to God's love. If we listen to our hearts, we will know who is in our basket of responsibility in a given moment.

Seeing with our souls nourishes a spiritual attitude. Or perhaps it is the other way around, and a spiritual attitude nourishes our capacity to see with our souls. The phrase "spiritual attitude" can easily be misunderstood. It does not mean pomposity and showy piety. It does not mean ignoring the complexity of today's

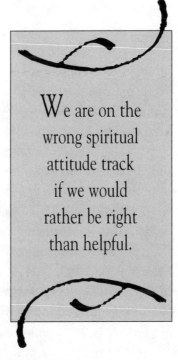

We are on the wrong spiritual attitude track if we would rather be right than helpful.

world. It does not mean limiting faith to a rigid set of "right" rules. We are on the wrong spiritual attitude track if we would rather be right than helpful.

Back in the fifth century, some "right rule" kind of folk came to see Abba Poemen, one of the desert fathers. "Tell us," they said, "when we see brothers dozing during the sacred office, should we pinch them so they will stay awake?"

The old man responded: "Actually, if I saw a brother sleeping, I would put his head on my knees and let him rest."

That is seeing with our souls. It is compassion. It is being a healing presence, a channel of blessing.

How much people need a healing presence! In his book *The Wounded Heart of God*, Andrew Sung Park speaks of *han*.[2] It is a Korean word that, roughly translated, means "the pain of being victimized." *Han* can be described as a physical wound, "the division of the tissue of the heart caused by abuse, exploitation, and violence. It is the wound to feelings and self-dignity." *Han* is a kind of pain that brings forth shame.

This kind of pain is universal—all of us have experienced it to a greater or lesser degree. But in severe situations, it can permeate the very core of a person's existence. Park says, "In the life of han-ridden people, the mode of han overwhelms the other types of human emotion and becomes a domineering spirit." He suggests that the healing of *han* calls for "the negation of the negation."

Recently I visited an elementary school. As I entered a classroom, I noticed that construction-paper sunflowers decorated the walls, and a student's baby picture was in the center of each flower. A boy named Faruch, a refugee from the Balkans, was at the science table watching some caterpillars. Another boy wanted his place and jeered, "Faruch, you can't always get your way!"

I've been in Gornji Vakuf, Faruch's hometown. Two-story homes line the streets—some scarred with bullet holes, others caved in from bombs. I've seen camouflaged tanks and soldiers, heard the shelling and the bombers overhead, as Faruch must have time and time again. I've listened to the stories of women in the Balkan refugee centers. Women whose possessions had been reduced to the little bundle they'd been able to carry. Women who

lived with awareness that their missing husbands or sons or fathers were
probably among those murdered,
their bodies thrown into mass graves.

Remember the sunflowers with
baby pictures decorating the classroom wall? The center of Faruch's
flower is empty. His mom couldn't
flee with the family albums.

*Faruch, you can't always get your
way!* I think he knows that. Faruch
shows us *han,* for he has known vic-
timization, violence, and negation.

Listening
is vital to
journeying in
compassion.

Listening is vital to journeying in compassion with one who is suf- *Compasionate listening*
fering. Brother David Steindl-Rast provides insight for us all when
he writes about the monastic vow of obedience:

> The real task is learning to listen. The very word obedience comes
> from *ob-audire,* which means to listen intently. Its opposite is to
> be utterly deaf, and the word for this is literally *ab-surdus.*
> Everything is absurd until we learn to listen to its meaning; until
> we become "all ears" in obedience.
>   In order to listen, you have to be silent.[3]

How contrary this is to our tendency to give advice to the suf-
ferer! We mean well. We want to help. But unasked-for advice
implies superiority and demonstrates our own impatience. We draw
conclusions before listening to the story.

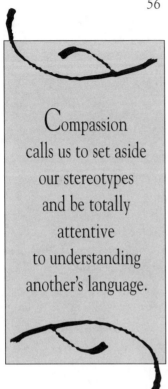

Compassion
calls us to set aside
our stereotypes
and be totally
attentive
to understanding
another's language.

Recently I was with a Volunteers in Mission group from the Dallas area who had been invited to attend a clergy retreat at Camp Poust, a United Methodist center in the Czech Republic. We sat outside under the trees on a beautiful afternoon. Dish towels hung over a fence to dry—plaid, checked, and striped in the colors of the clouds, leaves, and sky. One towel matched the bright marigolds that grew in wooden flower boxes. The tallest two pine trees were actually one, their divided trunks joined at the base and shared common roots. For me the merged trees served as God's visual reminder of the kind of partners our two areas wanted to become.

My friend Marcus was lecturing on the importance of listening in pastoral care. As he spoke, the sound of a keyboard, played by an eight-year-old boy, drifted out through the open window of his room. A baby cried. A duck quacked. The leaves danced with the sun as it traveled from one side of the double-trunked tree to the other as Marcus taught. His native language is German, and he was trying to make himself understood both by those who spoke Czech and those who spoke English. When he talked about the insensitivity of poor listening, he used the phrase "not right in our ears."

We want to be "right in our ears" when we journey with another person in compassion. Compassion calls us to set aside our stereotypes and be totally attentive to understanding another's language, that silent and anguished language of pain that longs for a response that will negate negation. It is as though we climb up a steep mountain, tethered together—not to carry the other, but to be a strong, gentle presence that can help break a fall.

WE need to stand on firm ground

Have you ever walked around a large sculpture or tree to look at it from different perspectives? That is part of what we do when we see with our souls: We broaden our perspective. For if our passion for one point of view deafens us to others, how can we hear the whisper of Mystery that teaches us compassion?

Zoom, by Istvan Banyai, is a wordless children's book on perception. It opens with a bright red drawing, jagged at the top. We assume that we see the whole picture. But we turn the page and our perception changes. What we thought was complete was merely part of a rooster's red comb. Page by page we realize that the image we hold is incomplete; it is merely a small part of something more. About halfway through the book, we discover that everything we have seen before is on a TV screen, watched by a man (turn the page), pictured on a stamp (turn the page), on a letter delivered to a person in another country. And so on. As our perspective broadens and our perception changes, we begin to understand that there is always something more beyond.

When we see with our souls, we look beyond a single, limited perspective, especially in world situations, for those who have the

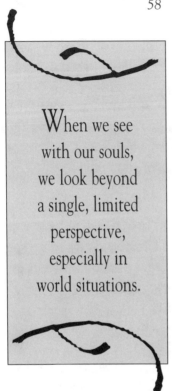

When we see with our souls, we look beyond a single, limited perspective, especially in world situations.

power to tell the story generally shape popular perceptions. And there is always something more beyond.

For an example, let's go back in time to the Native American tragedy, for now we can see it historically from a broader perspective than the headlines and newspaper accounts at the time. I know the Ute chapter in that tragedy best because of research I did for my novel *Crested Butte*. Chief Ouray was a proud man who was nearly broken by decades of his people's loss of land and pride and human dignity and the unhonored U.S. treaties that resulted in further loss of land and pride and human dignity. The story was repeated across our country. These peoples (who wanted the best for their families and were not bad folk) felt entitled to the land they'd held for centuries, at least the remaining territory ascribed to them by the latest U.S. treaty; settlers (who also wanted the best for their families and were not bad folk) felt entitled to encroach on that illegal territory.

A few of the angry dispossessed Native Americans committed vengeful acts of savagery, sometimes beyond their chief's control due to their opinion that he was too weak to protect his people. This violence begat violence, and the military defended the settlers,

using disproportionate force and collective punishment, indiscrim- ~~no~~
inately harming the innocent. Newspaper versions generalized ~~perspective~~
Indians as subhuman and disposable, portraying one image for all:
"Indian savage." And public sentiment, unconsciously accepting
that image, passionately condoned whatever force the U.S. military used to handle the Indian uprisings.

There were, of course, those in the United States who saw the
injustice and spoke out compassionately. But they were few—too
few. And the peoples who had lived on the land for centuries were
driven onto smaller and smaller pieces of the poorest areas, no
longer free to come and go as they pleased. It is a story that continues to haunt and disgrace us, for it is a story without compassion.

That story is being relived today in another part of the world.
For more than five decades a people have been losing their land
and their pride and their human dignity, and unhonored United
Nations resolutions have resulted in further loss of their land and
their pride and their human dignity. These people (who want the
best for their families and are not bad folk) feel entitled to the land
they've held for centuries, at least the remaining territory ascribed
to them by the latest United Nations resolutions; settlers (who also
want the best for their families and are not bad folk) feel entitled
to encroach on that illegal territory.

A few of the angry dispossessed commit vengeful acts of terror-
ism, sometimes beyond their leader's control due to their opinion
that he is too weak to protect his people. This violence begets
violence, and the military defends the settlers, using disproportionate force and collective punishment, indiscriminately harming
the innocent. News media versions generalize Palestinians as

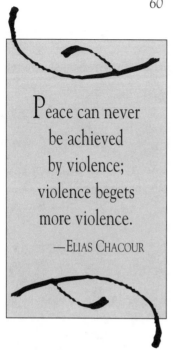

P eace can never
be achieved
by violence;
violence begets
more violence.

—ELIAS CHACOUR

subhuman and disposable, portraying one image for all: "Palestinian terrorist." And public sentiment, unconsciously accepting that image, passionately condones whatever force the Israeli military uses to handle the Palestinian uprisings.

There are, of course, those in Israel and those among the practicing Jews in our country who see the injustice and speak out compassionately. But they are few. Too few? Will this story end in a people who have lived in the Holy Land for centuries being continually driven onto smaller and smaller pieces of the poorest areas? Or driven out entirely? Will they continue to lose their freedom to come and go as they please? Will this too be a story that ends without compassion, a story that haunts and disgraces Israel? (And also our country, for once again the military weapons come from the U.S.—*us*.)

Father Elias Chacour is a Palestinian Christian priest who sees with his soul, for he tempers his passion for his people with compassion for all. He says: "Peace can never be achieved by violence; violence begets more violence. For the first time I saw clearly the face of my true enemy and the enemy of all who are friends of God and of peace: It was not the Zionists, but the demon of Militarism."4

Chacour dedicated his book *Blood Brothers* to "my brothers and sisters, the Jews who died in Dachau; and their brothers and sisters, the Palestinians who died in Tel-azzaatar, Sabra, and Shatila refugee camps." Chacour wrote that book nearly two decades ago. How long he has waited for Israelis and Palestinians alike to know peace in the land of the Prince of Peace! Yet, faithful to his call as peacemaker in the Middle East, he continues to see with his soul and hear the whisper of Mystery that speaks of compassion.

Throughout history irreligious leaders have misused religion to abet their own schemes for turf and power, inciting heinous violence in the holy name of God. The Balkans and the Middle East are merely recent examples. One thing we learn in looking at Jesus' life is that in his passion he showed compassion. When someone (including us) attempts to arouse religious passion in a way that excludes compassion, it is a ruse. We're being fooled or fooling ourselves—or both.

First Corinthians reminds us: "If one member suffers, all suffer together with it; if one member is honored, all rejoice together with it" (12:26). If one member of a family suffers intensely, it affects the whole family. So it is for the global family. National or individual isolationism is a veil of illusion in our global community. We are interconnected with one another, all God's creation and all God's creatures. Remember the Wise One? The dawn will come when we can see each person as our sister or our brother—those near to us and those in other parts of the world, those who believe as we do and those whose faiths differ from ours. The sun will rise when we no longer allow the people's side we take in passion to blind us to compassion for those on the other side of the sea, wall, river, street, or door.

We are interconnected with one sea, wall, river, street or door.

One of the major components of quantum theory—birthed by science, not spirituality—is interconnectedness. David Bohm describes our interconnectedness as "unbroken wholeness."[5] He says that we have "always been seeking wholeness—mental, physical, social, individual. The notion that all these fragments are separately existent is evidently an illusion" that leads to "conflict and confusion."[6] How we struggle for wholeness, for uniting the fragments of our lives! But suppose Bohm is right. Suppose we are born whole/holistic/holy, and our reactions to life experiences fragment that wholeness. Suppose that our life struggle is not to connect our separate parts but to reconnect the broken parts. Suppose that the same is true for the planet. Perhaps the game is not "Survival of the Fittest" after all but "Celebration of the Whole." The whole interconnected peoples and planet.

In quantum theory, things exhibit "nonlocal connection"—they are connected without the bond of connection. John B. Cobb Jr. and Charles Birch suggest that nothing occurs in isolation: "No event occurs without its interconnection with other events."[7] In another book Cobb suggests that "through all sorts of complex patterns all of us influence one another."[8] We participate in one

Butterfly effect

another's lives. For example, I had no local connection with Slobodan Milosevic, but he affected my life—through the instability he brought to the world (and earlier incidents in the Balkans had helped ignite both World Wars), through the pain of the Balkan people that I witnessed, and through my friend David who was a pilot in Kosovo.

In quantum theory, matter and energy have a dual nature and manifest either a wave or a particle, according to how they are treated. Likewise, we humans tend to respond according to how we are treated. That is true medically, psychologi-

physics

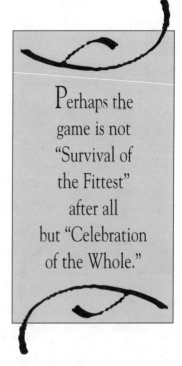

Perhaps the game is not "Survival of the Fittest" after all but "Celebration of the Whole."

cally, socially, and politically. It is even true in prison.

Bill and I visited a remarkable prison in the Czech Republic, where local United Methodists have a ministry. Though hardened criminals are sent there, the prison does not harden them further. They are treated with respect, many for the first time in their lives.

As we entered, I noticed that neither the guards nor the warden wore guns. There were no "prison" haircuts, uniforms, or cells. The prisoners were assigned to sections based on the severity of their crimes. They lived in unlocked dorm-style rooms that opened onto a large locked hall where they were free to socialize within their section.

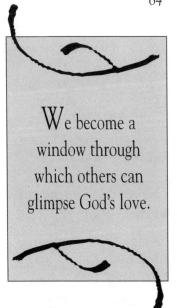

We become a window through which others can glimpse God's love.

Capital punishment is illegal in the Czech Republic, and the warden took us into the murder section. He and Bill and I mingled with murderers. The only guard—unarmed, remember—was a burly man at the entrance. It crossed my mind that we could be taken hostage, but I didn't feel afraid. These men, capable of murder, were friendly to us. They clearly respected the warden, yet engaged in easy conversation with him.

In a different section, a man proudly showed us a creative, well-designed truck he had made from empty tin cans for his two sons. In another, a young prisoner showed us a picture he had sketched of fish caught in a net in the Sea of Galilee. He said the picture had given him hope in prison. He was to be released the next week and wanted us to have it. Bill placed his hand on the young man's head, blessed him, and prayed for him. Tears came to his eyes (as they come to mine sometimes when I look at that picture and think of him and once again pray for him). Through the Christian warden and some Czech United Methodists, this young man experienced the healing presence of God's love, "the negation of the negation"—even in prison.

We are not always capable of seeing with our souls—of being an instrument of compassion, a healing presence, a channel of blessing. But at times we are, and those are precious times. In those moments we become a living icon of God, a window through which others can glimpse God's love. Often small children show us how. Our granddaughter Chelsea was three years old when Bill's father died. At the service she sat between Bill and me. Sensing his sorrow—listening to the language of his heart—she snuggled close to him, put her tiny hand on his, looked up at him, and whispered, "I love you, Granddad." She offered healing presence. In that moment she was a window to God's love.

Each day offers us an opportunity to journey in compassion with our sisters and brothers and, through God's grace, to be windows through which others can see God's love. When we experience God's transforming love and our lives reflect it, we see with our souls. And we glimpse what it means to live *abundantly*.

7

Stepping Out on Shifting Sands

See, I am doing a new thing!
Now it springs up;
do you not perceive it?

—Isaiah 43:19, NIV

We have considered community, calling, confession, choice of mind-set, and compassion. Basic to them all is confidence in God. Living abundantly is a journey on a spiritual labyrinth, remembering the commandments to love our neighbor as ourselves and to love God with all our heart, mind, and soul. And also with all our strength, which calls us to step out on the shifting sands of this strange new world, affirming Psalm 91:2: "My God, in whom I trust."

We are living through an unprecedented shift that the book *Connectionalism* calls a "time of great unsettlement."[1] The writers suggest that the question—"How shall I live?"—is still the same. But where to seek the answer has shifted away from the family, community, and local church. My life and perhaps yours span a

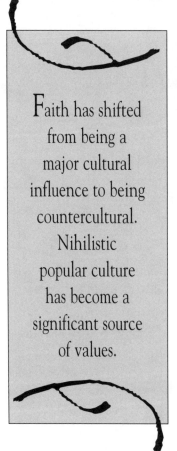

Faith has shifted from being a major cultural influence to being countercultural. Nihilistic popular culture has become a significant source of values.

time when faith has shifted from being a major cultural influence to being countercultural to what is popular in our country. Stepping out on these shifting sands requires bold confidence in God.

Thomas Hibbs suggests, "The worldview that best characterizes contemporary movies and television is nihilism," which he defines as "a state of spiritual impoverishment and shrunken aspirations." He notes the "growing sense that no religious or moral code is credible." This worldview, increasingly portrayed in movies, sees ultimate justice as elusive, and "violence and ineradicable guilt as the underlying truth about the human condition." It tempts us to see an underlying force that is malevolent and punitive.[2]

One result is the emergence of an unprecedented character, the demonic antihero. Hibbs cites *Silence of the Lambs* and Hannibal Lecter, played by Anthony Hopkins, as an example of a demonic antihero. This movie was so financially successful that its sequel, *Hannibal*, followed. Unlike movie heroes in the past, the demonic antihero revels in his freedom from moral constraints and invites the audience to celebrate his liberation.

Another result is despair, which is subtler but no less corrosive. Hibbs says this is best embodied in the comedy *Seinfeld*. He makes his point when he asks: "Have there ever been four more spiritually impoverished people than Jerry, Elaine, George, and Kramer? Did you ever see four people who aspired to less?" (Probably not!) According to Hibbs, the Seinfeld writers followed "two important rules: no hugs and no learning. The result was a world without any pretense to virtue, . . . where earnestness was nowhere to be found, and where the surface was all there was"—a nihilistic and godless world.

Roberto Rivera expresses his concern about the influence of nihilism in American popular culture.[3] He calls Eric Harris and Dylan Klebold "the children of Nietzsche." (To remember Harris and Klebold, think Columbine High School; to recall the work of Nietzsche, think: All is nothing.) Rivera describes their behavior as Nietzschean because they were tired of life, convinced there was nothing worth living for, knew that what they were about to do was wrong, and were "unconstrained by antiquated moral norms."

Rivera eliminates the causes generally set forth for Columbine: psychological factors, copycatting, and availability of guns. Instead, based on the videos Harris and Klebold made just before their rampage, he lifts up the role that American popular culture played in shaping their worldview: Harris told the camera that the shooting would be like *Doom*, his favorite video game—violent and gory. He named his gun Arlene after one of the game's characters. Harris and Klebold said on their video: "At least we will be

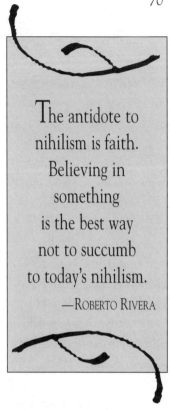

> The antidote to nihilism is faith. Believing in something is the best way not to succumb to today's nihilism.
>
> —ROBERTO RIVERA

remembered for the audacity and originality of our final actions."

Unfortunately, they were not the last youth to take this path. Rivera says that the antidote to nihilism is faith, that believing in something—in particular, God—is the best way not to succumb to today's nihilistic popular culture.

With the declining influence of the family and church, nihilistic popular culture has become a significant source of values. And because nihilism is marketed, it is reinforced, furthering its popularity. Among the results are an unapologetic "me-ism," a demonstrable lack of commitment, an apparent lack of honor, and the contagion of consumption. Without conscious consideration of our worldview and the place of faith in our lives, we relegate the gospel to the archives, and by default we and our children and grandchildren fall into the hands of the marketers of the godless.

A portion of the book *Connectionalism* deals with our reactions to this time of great unsettlement. The writers divide their study survey respondents into four "strategies of action"[4]:

1. Disenfranchised Pragmatists

To summarize briefly, if we are among the pragmatists, we focus on daily tasks and material things, avoid thinking much about what goes on in the world because we see it as beyond anyone's control, and follow consumerist rules. We are picky about energy spent on work and extravagant in our play. Attending church is a matter of convenience. I think of Pat.

I sat at Kuby's, a Dallas restaurant, revising this manuscript. Breakfast smells of coffee, bacon, and sausage wafted through the air, intermingling with customers' conversations. I chatted a moment with Steve (the best waiter in the business) and got back to work. Then the word *church* caught my attention, and I overheard the question "What do you think, Pat?"

The person called Pat, who shared the other side of the backrest of my booth, began to speak. "I went to church sometimes as a child. Didn't mean anything. It was just a front. Came away with images of heaven and hell, God on a throne with a scepter, and the devil in red with a pitchfork." Pat paused. "I don't believe any of that anymore."

The other person in the booth made some comments, and then Pat said, "I liked the social things. Went to camp once. The Bible stories had a good moral. But how can there be a God if you can't get a picture?"

Steve refilled the coffee, and I heard Pat once more, this time with a wistful tone. "Doesn't make much difference in my life one way or the other." Another pause. "You don't really need the church. You can go straight to the Boss."

2. Disaffected Skeptics

If this is where we fall, we deal with the anxieties of today's world by trying to lessen their emotional impact—through humor or a world-weary response or, most often, through intellectualizing. We feel tension between our desire to believe and our intellectual inability to believe, but we would like to be convinced. We focus on logic, discount the unprovable, and dare not risk the leap of faith. I remember an experience on a plane.

Seatmates cozied together on a Delta flight, Taylor and I exchanged first names and settled into our books. I was reading *Encounter with God's Love*, a small collection of the writings of Julian of Norwich.

I felt Taylor's eyes. "Interesting title."

I nodded. "Worth reading."

"I've thought a lot about religious issues. I used to be an atheist, but now I'm an agnostic."

I couldn't tell whether the pride in Taylor's voice came from being an agnostic or from moving away from being an atheist. "Ah," I said, borrowing Father Tim's noncommittal response in the Mitford series.

"I like to keep an open mind about God. But since there's no proof, I suppose you'll have to show me before I log on."

Doubting Thomas's descendant, right beside me. "I guess the sunrise is proof enough for me."

"The sunrise? Hmm. I can see where you're coming from on that." Taylor smiled. "I expected you to say that the Bible proves it. I don't trust the Bible. All those translators influenced by their culture and the politics of the situation. The King James Version of the Bible is probably just that—King James's version!"

I debated internally whether Taylor had fallen into my basket of responsibility during this flight or whether I could get back to Julian of Norwich.

"Do you know what I mean?"

I nodded.

"I like the idea of there being someone in control better than it just all being chaos. But the Spirit's never moved me!"

Taylor paused, an invitation for me to tell a Spirit story. But I felt this was not the time to take center stage—instead I needed to listen.

Taylor's voice softened. The edge of pride left. "It would be nice, though. Kind of comforting. Sometimes I think there may be something deeper. I'm living a pretty shallow life."

The flight attendant reached our row. "Something to drink?" The introspective mood was broke.

Taylor sipped sparkling water with a lime. "But look at the world. How could there be a God and all that awful stuff happen?"

3. Dislocated Idealists

If we fit in this group, we ignore the complexity of today's world instead of struggling with gray. We focus unrealistically on the "right way" to believe and behave and on the "right rules" to obey. We have an idealistic image of the church that does not match the reality and, therefore, it is not "good enough" for us; or we have an idealistic image of Christians and, therefore, we feel that we are not "good enough" for the church. When we are personally affected by a problem that doesn't allow strict adherence to our rigid rules, we tend to redefine the problem or subtly reinterpret the rules. I recall Chris.

I met Chris while leading a retreat enriched by persons with diverse views of faith. Chris was upset about some of the ideas expressed, and we took a walk beside a bayou. Spanish moss dripped from the limbs of the cypress trees.

"I have blind faith," proclaimed Chris. "Blind faith! God is Truth and truth is permanent. That's it. That's all. That's everything. How can they question?"

"God can handle questions, Chris," I said gently.

"There are no questions. There is God and Jesus and the Holy Spirit. The Bible tells us so. The King James. The real Bible. The Word of God! That's all you need. Nothing new. Nothing novel."

Chris stopped walking, and we watched the ducks. Two birds sang an antiphon.

"When I was a child, my mother got sick." Chris's voice came from a long-ago memory. "I prayed and prayed for her not to die. I asked, and I didn't receive. God called her home. He needed her in heaven. So he said no to me."

Chris turned from the bayou and looked at me, in the present once again. "Sometimes that happens. That's just the way it is. We can't mess with it."

I put my arm on Chris's shoulder, and we walked on in silence.

4. Activists and Disengaged Seekers

If we are in this category, we have a one-eyed focus either on activism or seeking. If we are activists, we mobilize resources to reduce the impact of today's problems, focusing on the outer world and ignoring the inner one. If we are seekers, we attempt to transcend the impact of today's problems, focusing on the spiritual world and ignoring the outer one. As seekers, we are spiritually oriented and liberal-minded, intolerant only of intolerance, and we abhor judgment, condemnation, and any type of guilt-motivated religion. We are likely to tell stories of vivid religious experiences that provided new insights and understandings that helped us make sense of our lives. Ryan comes to mind.

Ryan and I ended up in the same discussion group at a seminar on spiritual transformation. Ryan's easy smile and sense of humor were immediately likable. But there was no joking around when we talked about spirituality. Ryan spoke of his experience of seeing the Light. Literally.

Excitement filled Ryan's voice and eyes. "The pure Light! I *God moments* haven't seen it often. But in moments. Those are the best moments of my life."

Ryan intentionally chose a simple lifestyle, well guarded, no involvement in societal problems. "I cleared out the distractions. I want to learn how to live close to the Light. To be able to experience those moments more often. It's the most important thing to me, you know."

We could all see that.

"The first time I saw the Light, that's when healing began. If I have a dream, it's that everyone would know the joy of that Light."

Joy reflected in Ryan's eyes.

"I really like to be out in nature, you know. Somehow nature brings me closer to the center, to the Light." Ryan frowned. "I don't ever want to begin moving away from it, to forget it. If I have a fear, that's it."

For Ryan, the supernatural is a natural part of life.

The four categories of people mentioned in the above scenarios provide databased, broad-stroke glimpses of ways individuals react to this time of shift. The categories also demonstrate that our responses affect—and are affected by—our image of God. It is noteworthy that none of these categories is holistic. None seems to stem from an abundance worldview. None is adequate for this new day. Perhaps John Updike sums up the problem in *Self-Consciousness:* "Our brains are no longer conditioned for reverence and awe."

My experiences as a counselor helped me realize that each person is unique. Ability and personality tests, as well as study surveys, provide helpful personal or societal clues, but human beings can't be sorted into stacks like laundry or packed neatly into a certain number of boxes. Even if we do fit into a particular box, the lid is not locked. We are dynamic, not static, created with the freedom to choose and the capacity to change.

Like reading the book *Zoom,* we may think we have the whole God-picture and feel threatened when a new page is turned in our life or the world, a page that causes something new to clash against our old assumptions, a page that forces us either to hide our eyes or enlarge our concept of God. If our concept of God today is only as broad as it was yesterday, it won't be big enough for tomorrow.

Bishop Rueben Job says that it is "grace, coupled with our disciplined life, that leads to a life of peace, assurance, faithfulness, and usefulness"[5]—a life of abundance. Trusting God's grace and practicing the spiritual disciplines help us to continue turning the pages of faith, broadening our perspective and deepening our confidence in God's presence, reconditioning our brains for reverence and awe—even in this time of great unsettlement.

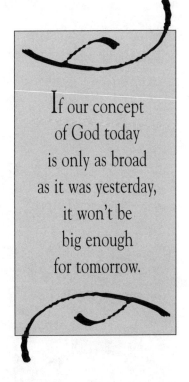

If our concept of God today is only as broad as it was yesterday, it won't be big enough for tomorrow.

In addition to the shift in the influence of the church, we also experience an unprecedented shift in our world order. Thomas Friedman, Pulitzer prize-winning journalist for the *New York Times*, says that we have entered into a new system of globalization that "constitutes a fundamentally new state of affairs."[6]

For example, technology enables "more and more people . . . to reach farther and farther, into more and more countries, faster and faster, deeper and deeper, cheaper and cheaper than ever before in history."[7] Now people do not have to depend on the infrastructure of mail systems, roads, or phone lines to communicate; and governments can't control the information that leaves or enters their country—digital cameras and written transmissions by computer

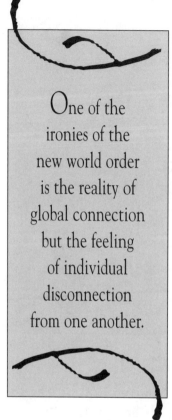

One of the ironies of the new world order is the reality of global connection but the feeling of individual disconnection from one another.

are not subject to checkpoints. One of the ironies of this new world order is the reality of global connection but the feeling of individual disconnection from one another.

In *The Lexus and the Olive Tree*, Friedman discusses the struggle between two forces. The Lexus represents dedication "to modernizing, streamlining and privatizing" economies in order to thrive in this new system of globalization. The olive tree represents "everything that roots us, anchors us, identifies us and locates us in this world—whether it is belonging to a family, a community, a tribe, a nation, a religion or, most of all, a place called home."[8] These forces are more conflictual than complementary, and we too feel their pull. We can choose to cling to the olive tree or to rev the Lexus. But our journey toward abundant living invites us to build bridges between the two. Globalization is new, but the old Word still speaks: "See, everything has become new! All this is from God, who reconciled us to himself through Christ, and has given us the ministry of reconciliation" (2 Cor. 5:17*b*-18).

When we try to understand the impact of globalization, we are staggered by its complexity—we turn on the computer screen of our minds, go into overload, and the hard drive crashes! Friedman suggests that we need to look through a multidimensional lens (politics, culture, and environment, for example) to gain understanding of each part of globalization. But even that is not enough to grasp the whole picture. The crux is being aware of the interaction between the parts, what is revealed and concealed through their subtle interplay and inevitable interconnections. Do you remember connect-the-dots books from your childhood? We have access to more "dots" than ever before, but we can't see the picture until we connect them. Says Friedman, "If you don't see the connections, you won't see the world."

Faith is central to our integration of globalization's complexities. My image is to put away our glasses and pick up a special kaleidoscope. The first lens—the one closest to the eye—is a faith lens. As we look at the many dimensions of globalization through the lens of faith, we see their bright colorful pieces turn with the world, constantly interacting and reshaping their patterns. Rather than overwhelming us, this lens gives us a holistic view and invokes our gratitude for the dynamic beauty we see.

If we learn nothing else from Friedman, he teaches us the futility of single perspectives, narrow views, and simplistic opinions. No matter how loudly we shout in their defense, they remain ineffective and impede reconciliation. Perhaps the best we can do is to be aware of the necessity for multiple international perspectives, to realize that we are part of the system of globalization, and to focus in a new way on our small bit of the world. Merton tells us: "We are able to decide whether we ourselves, and that portion of the world which is ours, shall become aware of His presence, consecrated by it, and transfigured in its light."[9] As we grow in faith, we are "renewed in knowledge according to the image of its creator" (Col. 3:10). This faith roots us in our spiritual connection and gives us bold confidence in God so we can step out on the shifting sands as reconcilers in this new world order.

On that terrible Tuesday of September 2001, Americans experienced one of the most unsettling acts ever to occur within our country's borders. Terrorists struck our symbols of economic security and military superiority. And thousands of innocent people died. We felt numbed by disbelief, unable to fathom such premeditated malevolence. We joined the rest of the world in knowing what it is to feel vulnerable on our own soil.

The fire, police, and disaster crews shook us awake with their courage, patience, and unwavering commitment. We hurt for the victims from around the world who were trapped in planes and on the ground. We hurt for their families. We hurt for our country. Anger rose within our hearts against the power-hungry, hate-filled megalomaniacs who distorted and misused faith, warping it into a weapon of manipulation for satanic acts—surely the greatest evil of all! But side by side with anger stood compassion. The impact of that terrible Tuesday hit the most logical head and shriveled heart. Patriotism and unity were reborn. Our national spirit was not quashed but enlivened.

That was something Osama bin Laden couldn't predict. He and his cronies could mastermind every-thing except the response of the American people. They miscalcu-lated a people whose government empowers them rather than sup-presses them, a people whose country was birthed by courage and founded on principles of freedom, equality, and the rights of the governed, a people who live together in won-drous diversity. Such a people are not known for cowering in the face of adversity!

In the roar of disbelief and anguish came a whisper that drew us toward prayer and special services in chapels and sanctuaries, synagogues and mosques. We sang patriotic reli-gious songs that we hadn't sung in decades. We sang them with a new understanding and with gratitude, and our eyes brimmed with tears. Feeling vulnerable, we set aside "political correctness" and, individually and as a nation, we invoked aloud and unashamedly the name of God. We who are sons and daughters of the three Abrahamic faiths (Judaism, Christianity, and Islam) stood together, reclaiming faith and proclaiming the one holy God.

> Feeling vulnerable (in the aftermath of September 11) we set aside political correctness and invoked aloud and unashamedly the name of God.

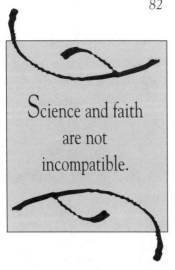

Science and faith are not incompatible.

Perhaps Rivera is right about faith being the antidote to nihilism. (See pages 69–70.) Both life and death have been washed in new meaning. On his first show after that terrible Tuesday, even David Letterman, who has grasped the nihilistic bent of the people for years, spoke sincerely of meaning—and received applause from the audience. It remains to be seen whether we will fall back totally into old attitudes and behaviors or alter them to some degree. But we cannot be exactly the same, for we have been awakened. Even if we nod off again, the memory is lodged in our minds—not only the terrorist acts but also the courageous aftermath with its new vision. For the moment at least, nihilism toppled with the twin towers.

A shift in science has also occurred in this time of great unsettlement. Today's science sounds like science fiction. We are fearful of what science can now do. We wonder if we have stepped into God's domain. Yet, do we really believe that God finds ignorance more worshipful than knowledge? Or can science and faith be compatible?

Francis Collins, head of the Human Genome Project when the

genetic code was broken, shared his insight during a television interview.[10] He said that he was not exposed to religion as a child and was an atheist in college. But at age twenty-seven he read *Mere Christianity* by C. S. Lewis and took the leap of faith. Now his faith is a driving force in his life. He believes in God as creator and commented that 40 percent of the world's most respected scientists join him in this belief. He thinks that science and faith are not incompatible, for science explores the natural, and faith explores the spiritual. He sees factual truth as part of God's creation.

Unlike Collins, we are strangers to this new world of genomics. Cracking the genetic code threatens us. We don't want to hear that those we dislike because they are so "different" are actually quite similar—for genetically, human beings are 99.9 percent alike! And we are quite disturbed that all God's creatures, great and small, are very much alike—that the genetics of humans, animals, plants, and viruses are similar. (Viruses?!) There are more differences within these groups than between them. What a comeuppance! But the human genome is mapped. The biotech age is upon us. Denial won't work.

A couple of years ago I attended a futurist seminar led by Richard Oliver, author of *The Coming Biotech Age*.[11] As he talked about biotech research for new products, I felt like an alien on my own planet:

- ❧ Bats, skis, and bikes designed to absorb shock by converting mechanical energy to electrical energy.
- ❧ New paints designed for insulation by storing the sun's energy in cold weather and repelling heat in hot weather.

- ∾ Genetically altered bacteria designed to clean up pollution.
- ∾ Trees designed for industry and capable of full growth in a few years rather than a hundred, and perhaps in some cases even designed to manufacture themselves into finished products.
- ∾ Christmas trees designed to grow with a glow, appearing to have their own lights.
- ∾ A natural plant designed as a substitute for the raw materials in plastic, instead of relying on oil.
- ∾ Grass designed to stay the same height so we don't have to mow.
- ∾ And, vegetarians, how about this one? Grass designed to become steak without the messy middle stage of a cow—in order to help feed the masses.

Some of this research threatens us. We prefer to dance to the beat of an antique drum. We forget that genetic engineering is not new. It entered the animal kingdom about a thousand years before Christ, when a farmer crossbred a female horse with a male donkey to create the mule. Genetically altered edible plants have been around since growers tampered with maize to produce different kinds of corn. There is no doubt, however, that the increasing capabilities of science call for guidance from a deeper source than profit. Perhaps that is why it was important to Francis Collins to keep genomic matters in the public domain rather than the corporate one.

Oliver's twists also included some interesting medical predictions. For example, potatoes designed to contain childhood vaccines. He told about a woman who is spending her life working on this project. Since potatoes are a common food around the globe, this would be an affordable way to inoculate the world's poor against diseases. Another prediction is the ability to grow replacement parts (instead of using artificial ones) for people who are in accidents or have diseased body parts.

And finally, life expectancy. Oliver said that in Shakespeare's time, Juliet at thirteen had already reached midlife. At the beginning of the last century, life expectancy had nearly doubled, reaching forty-seven. Now, a life expectancy of 125 is just around the corner. And, according to Oliver, today's babies' babies could have an opportunity to live . . . indefinitely!

Richard Oliver is *not* a churchman. However, during the seminar he called on the religious communities for leadership: "You are the only ones who are global in your concern and have no vested interests. You alone transcend national, political, and economic agendas." His eyes scanned the room, and he asked, "Otherwise, who will speak for God?"

This new world has amazing opportunities for good but also an enormous capacity for evil. Wise and moral guideposts are desperately needed. In *Blood Brothers*, Elias Chacour shares the challenge of one of his professors at the Seminary of Saint Sulpice in Paris, who said that if there is a problem somewhere, 3 people will try to do something concrete to settle the issue, 10 people will give a lecture analyzing what the 3 are doing, 100 people will commend or

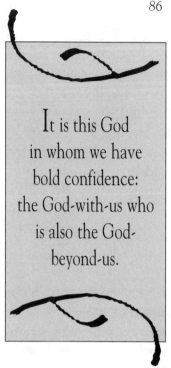

It is this God in whom we have bold confidence: the God-with-us who is also the God-beyond-us.

condemn the 10 for their lecture, 1000 people will argue about the problem. "And one person—only one—will involve himself [or herself] so deeply in the true solution that he [or she] is too busy to listen to any of it." Then the professor asked, "Which person are you?"[12] Where do we find ourselves? In what areas would we like to step out on these shifting sands but let the hopelessness of the situation deter us?

Throughout history there have been individuals who in their own small and undramatic way refused to be bearers of a disease of the spirit, refused to contribute to the capacity of evil, refused to be content with amoral vision, refused to be herded by a lack of wisdom, refused to wade through the sewage of the sin of omission. Brother Roger affirms the capacity of believers to make a difference: "Hoping against all hope, advancing towards the wellsprings of faith, believers change the course of certain evolutions of human history even without being very numerous."[13]

But changing the status quo is a great challenge. When a new perspective or idea or capability threatens us, we tend to act as though God prefers ignorance. Instead of stepping out with bold confidence in God and struggling to develop guideposts that transcend our vested interests, we tend to adopt a bunker mentality. Fearful, we oppose this new thing and assure ourselves that God also opposes it. We self-righteously cry, "Sacrilege!" and vociferously defend our narrow concept of God.

Just as readers experiencing the book *Zoom*, we assume that we grasp the whole God-picture. But our perception of God is incomplete. It will never be complete. There will always be something more, something outside our vision, something beyond our capacity for understanding. It is this God in whom we have bold confidence, the God-with-us who is also the God-beyond-us. Nouwen said, "When we know that God holds us safely—whatever happens—we don't have to fear anything or anyone but can walk through life with great confidence."[14]

God Box

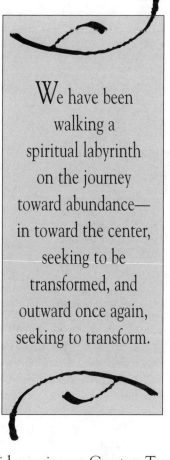

We have been walking a spiritual labyrinth on the journey toward abundance— in toward the center, seeking to be transformed, and outward once again, seeking to transform.

These shifting sands call us as persons of faith to step out in bold confidence in our Creator. To break free from fear and embrace leadership in this crucial time. To go up to Mount Sinai and, like Moses, come down with moral guideposts for this complex new millennium.

Otherwise, who will speak for God?

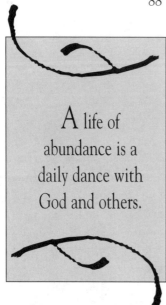

A life of abundance is a daily dance with God and others.

We have been walking a spiritual labyrinth on the journey toward living abundantly. Going in toward the center, seeking to be transformed. And then going outward once again, seeking to transform. To be transformed and to transform: This is our rhythm. This is our dance.

Abundance—both the word and the way ends in *dance*. Wallace Chappell, a retired associate pastor of First United Methodist Church in Dallas, proclaimed in a powerful sermon:

> Listen to me: I do not live an hour without physical pain. I do not live a day without the heartbreak of dreams unfulfilled, sins remembered, and a sense of longing for what might have been but will never be. I will soon be eighty. I know I am in my twilight years. But I know the goodness of life, the blessedness of God's love; for I have heard the God who speaks within my thoughts, and I cannot be separated from that love. . . . I know I cannot envision so beautiful a creation without so wonderful a Creator.

Wally Chappell knows the identity of his partner in the abundance of life.

A life of abundance is a daily dance with God and others. For God whispers to us:

Will you dance with me?

And will you dance with the little Faruchs who are strangers in a new land?

Will you dance with those in prison and the sick at heart?

Will you dance with the lonely and clothe them with love?

Will you dance with those who thirst for meaning in our nihilistic culture?

Will you dance with those who hunger for bread?

Will you dance onto the shifting sands of this new age and help speak for me?

And the people of <u>faith</u> respond . . .

Guide for Groups

A Word to Leaders

As leader, you have six major responsibilities:

1. To begin and end each session on time.

2. To make the weekly reading assignment clear.

3. To follow the guide when appropriate for the group but not to see it as an "assignment" to be accomplished. The Holy Spirit provides the rhythm for this dance together. The questions are merely discussion starters.

4. To facilitate group sharing so that no one dominates but everyone has equal opportunity to share without feeling pressured to do so. (A group of ten people would mean that each person's fair share—including the leader's—is 10 percent of the time allotted.)

5. To set the tone for the sessions as a warm, comfortable, and stimulating place to be. A centering symbol might help; for example, lighting a candle and opening a Bible and placing those items at the center of a table.

6. To close each session on a hopeful, accepting, caring note.

Since each person is a unique creation of God, we celebrate our differences rather than fear them. Though our silence together may feel a bit uneasy in the beginning, we will become more comfortable with it as the adventure continues.

The Weekly Guide is set up for a seven-week journey together. If you plan an eight-week journey, use the first session to help participants become acquainted with one another and to introduce the book and the format. For a six-week journey, get the books to the participants in advance and ask them to read chapters 1 and 2 before the first session; you may want to try to set up the first meeting as a longer session. *Prepare ahead for the Session 7 closing.* With the special closing and the long chapter, you may want to set up the last meeting as a longer session also.

A WORD TO PARTICIPANTS

Abundance is a journey together. We dance with one another and with God. The Spirit provides the rhythm. Our dance together is one of support and accountability. It includes:

- ∾ praying daily for one another
- ∾ reflecting on a scripture
- ∾ reading the designated section of *Abundance*
- ∾ viewing each session as a sacred opportunity for spiritual growth
- ∾ being open to the Spirit's leading
- ∾ expecting this dance together to make a difference in our journey toward abundant living

Agree to honor these community courtesies:

ぬ To listen in love, without disapproving other "dancers" and to share in truth (as we perceive it).

ぬ To value individual uniqueness and to welcome fresh perspectives, recognizing that the richness of diversity helps us grow.

ぬ To face differences openly, treating one another with respect and applying the Revised Standard Version's translation of Isaiah 1:18—"Come now, let us reason together"— rather than the New Revised Standard Version's "Come now, let us argue it out"!

ぬ To honor requests for confidentiality.

Guide for a Retreat

A Word to Leaders" and "A Word to Participants" (pages 91–93) also apply to a retreat setting. Retreat participants need to read the book prior to the retreat. Repeat the following outline for each session, adapting it based on the length of the retreat and the interests of the participants:

CENTERING THROUGH SILENCE AND PRAYER

There are many ways to pray:

- ∾ Silently centering ourselves individually.

- ∾ Repeating a breath prayer, for example: "Lord Jesus Christ" [inhale], . . . "have mercy on me" [exhale].

- ∾ Saying the Lord's Prayer together.

- ∾ Inviting individuals to pray.

- ∾ Inviting the group to pray spontaneously as desired.

READING THE SCRIPTURE

- ∾ You may want to reflect on the Great Commandment (Matt. 22:37-38; Mark 12:29-30; Luke 10:25-28) or on the scripture at the beginning of each chapter, as appropriate for the group and as time allows.

- ∾ Feel free to choose other scriptures that would be meaningful to participants and relevant to living abundantly.

- ∾ You could also adapt the Aramaic version of the Beatitudes found in the Weekly Guide. (See "Introduction" [pages

97–98] and "Rethinking a Familiar Scripture" [found in each weekly session].)

The scripture can be read in many ways. Here are a few ideas:

∾ Read the scripture as though it is the first time you have ever had the privilege to do so. Until Gutenberg's invention (mid-1400s), Bibles were hand-copied and rare. Christians have had personal access to the Bible only in relatively recent times.

∾ Repeat a word or phrase from the scripture, pondering it and resting in it.

∾ Read the scripture as though it is a personal word to you.

∾ Read the scripture seeking different levels of meaning.

∾ Reflectively meditate on the scripture by considering:
   What does this mean to me?
   Where does this apply to my life?
   How do I respond?

REFLECTING AND SHARING

Discuss passages from the book. Questions in the Weekly Guide for each chapter may be helpful.

REJOICING IN GOD'S GIFTS

Close each session by providing an opportunity for each person (who desires) to share a simple gift of God received since arriving at the retreat. It might be something tangible (something seen in nature) or something intangible (feeling a sense of belonging or of feeling close to God).

Returning to God's World with Prayerful Hearts
(at the close of the final session)

Plan a special closing for the retreat that involves everyone, celebrates God's grace, focuses on gratitude, and offers an opportunity to experience abundance of life in a way that is appropriate and meaningful for the participants. Be creative and trust the Spirit!

Weekly Guide

INTRODUCTION

One ingredient of living abundantly is to risk the discomfort of looking at the familiar in a new way—not dismissing the familiar but opening ourselves to new possibilities through new awareness. It can be exciting because of broadening our vision with a new "Aha!" But it can also be uncomfortable by threatening our accustomed view.

For example, our image of Jesus is typically influenced by paintings like *Jesus Knocking at the Door* and Sallman's *Head of Christ*. It is a rare American or European Christian whose image of Christ is a Middle Eastern Jesus.

Language interpretation offers another example. Jesus would have known temple Hebrew, but the common cultural language of Palestine was Aramaic, from which Arabic evolved. As Jesus walked through the Palestinian landmarks we know about from the New Testament, he used Aramaic to talk to the people around him, tell his stories, and proclaim the good news. Some scholars maintain that the books of Matthew and Luke were drawn from an Aramaic document known as "Q" (*Quelle*, meaning "source" in German). Others believe that Matthew was first written in Aramaic. Perhaps supporting this view is the fact that the Jewish historian Josephus, a Palestinian Jew born shortly after the Crucifixion, wrote his first work (*History of the Jewish War*) in

Aramaic, and parts of the Hebrew scriptures, some of the Dead Sea
Scrolls, and many rabbinical stories were also written in Aramaic.
Regardless, our familiar English versions of Matthew were translated from Greek, not Aramaic. Despite efforts to be faithful to the
text, translated material is unavoidably influenced by the translators' culture. Jesus' Aramaic words were filtered through Greek culture, politics, and worldview. The Palestinian common reference
points and cultural subtleties, color and complexity, energy and
earthiness were coated with the ethos, mores, and morality of the
Greeks. Cultural influence on a translation can result to some
degree in using the correct words but perhaps missing the spirit—
this is like playing all the right notes but missing the rhythm; or
dancing the steps in the proper sequence learned by the head but
missing the gracefulness of the heart.

"Rethinking a Familiar Scripture" provides an opportunity in
each session to look at a familiar verse from Matthew in a new way.
In *Prayers of the Cosmos: Meditations on the Aramaic Words of Jesus*,
Neil Douglas-Klotz offers us an interpretation of the Beatitudes
based on Aramaic. He explains that because an Aramaic word
offers more than one translation, a passage could be translated "literally" using several meanings. For example, each beatitude begins
with the Aramaic word *tubwayhun*, and he translates it as
"blessed," as well as "healthy," "healed," "integrated," "resisting
delusion," and "tuned to the Source." He also reminds us of the
commonalities of language origins in all three Abrahamic faiths
(Judaism, Christianity, and Islam). For example, the ancient word
for God was *El* or *Al*, a root we see in the Hebrew *Elohim*, the
Aramaic *alaha*, and the Arabic *Allah*. As we look at the familiar in

a new way, we will practice risking discomfort, and perhaps we will also open ourselves to the joy of an "aha!" experience.

Session 1
Seeking the Secret

Connecting with One Another

Help the group become acquainted with one another. You may want to go around the circle, giving the name you prefer to be called, and sharing in a word what the book cover brings to mind. It might be helpful to go around the circle once more, again saying your name and sharing briefly something you look forward to in this journey together.

- Introduce the book and the format for the group.
- Read "A Word to Participants," page 92, adjusting it as appropriate for your group.

Centering through Silence and Prayer

For suggestions for ways to pray, see Guide for a Retreat, page 94.

Begin this part with a centering symbol if you chose one. (See "A Word to Leaders," page 91.)

Reflecting and Sharing

Discuss chapter 1.

- What are some popular answers to the question of where to seek abundant life?

∽ What are some of the things that we give our hearts to that don't bring us a sense of satisfaction and fulfillment?

∽ When Jesus talked about abundant life, he was not referring to having many possessions. But often we confuse abundant living with having material possessions. Why do you think that is true?

∽ Name some things that give you a sense of chaos. Name things that give you a sense of order.

∽ Have you ever walked a spiritual labyrinth? If so, describe that experience.

∽ How does achievement differ from awakening?

RETHINKING A FAMILIAR SCRIPTURE

Review the introduction to the Weekly Guide.

Now, let's look at the first beatitude as it relates to seeking to live abundantly:

Blessed are the poor in spirit, for theirs is the kingdom of heaven. (Matt. 5:3)

∽ The word translated as "poor" is *meskenaee* in Aramaic and may relate to holding on to something in a devoted way, clinging to it because we would feel "poor" without it.

∽ The word translated as "spirit" is *rukh* in Aramaic and may also mean "breath" or "soul" or something that animates us, linking us to life.

∽ The word translated as "heaven" is *d'ashmaya* in Aramaic. Its roots *shm* and *aya* relate to rising and shining in space, a shining that is all-encompassing, including potential abilities. In other words, we might say that the universe itself is a way we recognize God.

One version of the first beatitude, translated from Aramaic, is this:

> Blessed are those who devotedly hold fast to the spirit of life; holding them is the cosmic Ruler of all that shines and rises.[1]

1. Read the familiar translation from Greek of the first beatitude, followed by the version based on Aramaic. What similarities and differences do you notice?

2. What does the Aramaic version of this beatitude say to you about living abundantly?

3. You may want to compare your visual image of Jesus with your image of the Semitic Palestinian people (native Jews, Christians, and Muslims). Is it difficult to picture the Palestinian Jesus? If so, why?

REJOICING IN GOD'S GIFTS

Give each person (who desires) an opportunity to share a simple gift of God received this day. It might be something tangible (something seen in nature) or something intangible (feeling a sense of belonging or of being close to God).

RETURNING TO GOD'S WORLD WITH PRAYERFUL HEARTS

Take turns praying for one another. You may want to stand in a circle and suggest that each person pray for the individual on his or her right.

REMAINING CONNECTED

~ Throughout the week, hold in your heart the person for whom you prayed.

~ Remember to reflect on scripture and pray daily for one another.

~ Read chapter 2 before the next session.

Session 2
LONGING FOR BELONGING

RECONNECTING WITH ONE ANOTHER

Reflect on these questions:

~ When did you most feel the presence of God this week?

~ When did you least feel the presence of God this week?

CENTERING THROUGH SILENCE AND PRAYER

Begin this part with a centering symbol if you chose one.

REFLECTING AND SHARING

Discuss chapter 2.

~ Think about the word *we*. Who makes up some important parts of "we" for you?

~ What comes to mind when you hear the word *home?* What does "home" mean to you?

∾ Have you ever moved and had to find a new church home? Was it difficult or easy? Why? How does that experience help you in welcoming newcomers who visit your church?

∾ Think of some times or places when you experienced belonging. You may want to share one.

∾ Share an experience when you and another (or others) to whom you were committed focused together on something beyond yourselves.

∾ Have you ever experienced a synergetic force (the power of the Spirit) in a group? If so, you may want to share it.

RETHINKING A FAMILIAR SCRIPTURE

Recall that one ingredient in abundant living is risking the discomfort of looking at something familiar in a new way. Consider the seventh beatitude in relation to community (if needed, look again at the Introduction to the Weekly Guide):

Blessed are the peacemakers, for they will be called children of God. (Matt. 5:9)

∾ The word translated "peacemakers" is two words in Aramaic: *shlama* and *lahwvday*. Essentially, *shlama* served as a Middle Eastern greeting. It also relates to safety and health, as well as the unification of all parties in sympathy. *Lahwvday* relates not just to acting (for example, "making" peace) but also to commitment to the action, to doing something regularly regardless of the odds.

∾ The words translated "will be called" and "children" are *nitqarun* and *dawnaw(hie)* in Aramaic. The roots of the word *nitqarun* evoke the image of digging water (perhaps a channel). *Dawnawhie* connotes the embodiment or production of something that previously was merely potential. As we act in peace, our actions ripple toward fulfillment of God's will.

One version of the seventh beatitude, translated from Aramaic, is this:

> *Blessed are those who bear the fruit of sympathy and safety for all; they shall hasten the coming of God's new creation.*[2]

1. Read the familiar translation from Greek of the seventh beatitude, followed by the version based on Aramaic. What similarities and differences do you notice?

2. What does the Aramaic version of this beatitude say to you about life in community?

3. What does it say about living your own life abundantly?

REJOICING IN GOD'S GIFTS

Give each person (who desires) an opportunity to share a simple tangible or intangible gift of God received this day.

RETURNING TO GOD'S WORLD WITH PRAYERFUL HEARTS

Go around the circle and pray (by name) for the person on your left.

REMAINING CONNECTED

∾ Throughout the week, hold in your heart the person for whom you prayed.

∾ Remember to reflect on scripture and pray daily for one another.
∾ Read chapter 3 before the next session.

Session 3
Yearning and Discerning

Reconnecting with One Another

Reflect on these questions:
∾ When did you most feel the presence of God this week?
∾ When did you least feel the presence of God this week?

Centering through Silence and Prayer

Begin this part with a centering symbol if you chose one.

Reflecting and Sharing

Discuss chapter 3.
∾ Have you ever felt like a character in someone else's life story?
∾ Reflect on whether the life you are living is the life that wants to live in you. You may want to share your thoughts.
∾ Do you ever feel that your identity is divided?
∾ What is "bread" for you? What do you feel is your deepest calling?
∾ Why are we afraid to listen to our dissatisfactions?

- ∾ Reflect on whether you need to do something differently—to make some change—that will keep you from looking back and mourning this time in your life. You may want to share your thoughts.
- ∾ We are all unfinished poems. What verse do you hope to write in the near or distant future?

RETHINKING A FAMILIAR SCRIPTURE

The second beatitude is probably not one we would relate to our calling in its familiar translation from Greek:

Blessed are those who mourn, for they will be comforted. (Matt. 5:4)

However, we get another point of view when we consider a version based on Aramaic.

- ∾ The word translated "mourners" is *lawile* in Aramaic and also relates to people who are troubled, who have a deep longing for something to happen.
- ∾ The word translated "comforted" is *netbayun* in Aramaic and also relates to a sense of inner continuity, of seeing something you long for, of returning from wandering.

One version of the second beatitude, translated from Aramaic, is this:

Blessed are those who weep for their frustrated desire; they shall see the face of fulfillment in a new form.[3]

1. Compare the Greek and Aramaic versions of the second beatitude. What are their similarities and differences?

2. What does the Aramaic version of this beatitude say to you about finding meaning in your life?

3. What does it say to you about discerning your calling and living it out?

REJOICING IN GOD'S GIFTS

Give each person (who desires) an opportunity to share a simple tangible or intangible gift of God received this day.

RETURNING TO GOD'S WORLD WITH PRAYERFUL HEARTS

Go around the circle and individually pray for yourselves, both a prayer of petition for something you want and a prayer of thanksgiving for something for which you are grateful. (That's harder than it sounds for many of us!)

REMAINING CONNECTED

- ～ Throughout the week, hold in your heart your own desire for "bread," and nurture that desire to be fed with a sense of meaning and purpose.
- ～ Remember to reflect on scripture and pray daily for one another.
- ～ Read chapter 4 before the next session.

Session 4
HEALING OUR HEARTS

RECONNECTING WITH ONE ANOTHER

Reflect on these questions:

- ～ When did you most feel the presence of God this week?
- ～ When did you least feel the presence of God this week?

CENTERING THROUGH SILENCE AND PRAYER

Begin this part with a centering symbol if you chose one.

REFLECTING AND SHARING

Discuss chapter 4.

- ～ Why are we afraid to admit that we have a shadow side?
- ～ Look at each of the eight frailties that Evagrius named. Reflect on which one(s) cause you the most difficulty. You may want to share your thoughts.
- ～ How can you bring yourself to trust God to love you, shadow side and all?
- ～ If you have a spiritual guide or have had one in the past, share how it was a helpful (or unhelpful) experience.

RETHINKING A FAMILIAR SCRIPTURE

Let's look at the fourth beatitude in relation to healing our hearts:

Blessed are those who hunger and thirst for righteousness, for they will be filled. (Matt. 5:6)

Again, we might question how the translation from Greek fits with healing our hearts; and again, the version from Aramaic offers new meaning.

- ∞ The word translated "those" is *layleyn* in Aramaic. Its roots relate to waiting in the night, evoking an image of watchfulness in the lamplight while encircled by darkness, waiting with a sense of expectancy and anticipation rather than fear. We can identify with a sense of desire that in itself creates a possibility.

- ∞ The word translated "hunger" is *d'kaphneen* in Aramaic. It means "the hungering" and also relates to longing to strengthen ourselves physically.

- ∞ The word translated "thirst" is *tzheyn* in Aramaic and calls forth the image of being dried out, parched inwardly (like feeling burned out).

- ∞ The word translated "righteousness" is *khenuta* in Aramaic and includes "a sense of physical, inner rightness among the different voices we sometimes feel within."[4] It also relates to reflections of these voices in our outer world.

- ∞ The word translated "filled" is *nisbhun* in Aramaic. It means "satisfied" and also incorporates the image of being "surrounded by fruit," "encircled by birthing," and "embraced by generation."[5] This sowing/reaping image is common in Jesus' teachings.

One version of the fourth beatitude, translated from Aramaic, is this:

> *Blessed are those who long clearly for a foundation of peace between the warring parts of themselves; they shall find all around them the materials to build it.*[6]

1. Compare the versions of the fourth beatitude. What are their similarities and differences?

2. What does this beatitude say to you as you reflect on your own shadow side, your weaknesses from Evagrius's list, and your own warring parts?

Rejoicing in God's Gifts

Give each person (who desires) an opportunity to share a simple tangible or intangible gift of God received this day.

Returning to God's World with Prayerful Hearts

∼ Spend a few minutes in silence in your closing circle and give each person (who desires) an opportunity to share a "frailty" that he or she would like to begin healing. (No names are to be called or any kind of pressure placed on anyone.)

∼ Go around the circle and pray (by name) for the person to your right, praying specifically for help in the area named (or generally if no "frailty" was mentioned).

Remaining Connected

∼ Hold in your heart the person to your right and pray daily for his or her desired change.

∼ Remember to reflect on scripture and pray daily for one another.

∼ Read chapter 5 before the next session.

Session 5
REVIEWING OUR WORLDVIEW

RECONNECTING WITH ONE ANOTHER

Reflect on these questions:

- When did you most feel the presence of God this week?
- When did you least feel the presence of God this week?

CENTERING THROUGH SILENCE AND PRAYER

Begin this part with a centering symbol if you chose one.

REFLECTING AND SHARING

Discuss chapter 5.

- Share an example of the scarcity mind-set that you have seen in (unnamed) individuals.
- Think about whether you have seen examples of a scarcity mind-set in a church. You may want to give one example.
- Share an example of the abundance mind-set that you have seen in (unnamed) individuals.
- Think about whether you have seen examples of an abundance mind-set in a church. You may want to give one example.
- Reflect on a time when you chose to have a good attitude about a difficult situation. You may want to share your thoughts.

～ Reflect on whether wrong choices have sometimes turned out to be beneficial to you. You may want to share your thoughts.

～ Do you tend to focus on the *What if?*s or the *Wow!*s?

～ How do consumerism and marketing affect your decisions?

～ Paul said to be transformed by the *renewing of our minds*. How does renewing our minds help transform us so that we are not conformed to this world?

～ Reflect on the differences between an abundance image of God and a scarcity image of God. You may want to share your thoughts.

～ Share a time when you thought you had the whole story and then learned you had only a small part of it.

RETHINKING A FAMILIAR SCRIPTURE

Let's reflect on the third beatitude in relation to our own scarcity/ abundance worldviews, once again opening ourselves to seeing it in a new way:

Blessed are the meek, for they will inherit the earth. (Matt. 5:5)

～ The word translated "meek" is *l'makikhe* in Aramaic, relating to being humble or gentle. Among the connotations of the old roots is softening an area of inner hardness.

～ The word translated "inherit" is *nertun* in Aramaic and relates to "receiving from the universal source of strength."[7] In other words, as we soften our inner rigidities, we become more open to the power of God who acts through all nature (earthiness).

One version of the third beatitude, translated from Aramaic, is this:

> Blessed are those who have softened what is rigid within; they shall receive physical vigor and strength from the universe.[8]

1. Compare the Greek and Aramaic versions of the third beatitude. What are the similarities and differences?

2. What does the Aramaic version say to you in terms of your own worldview?

3. Share an experience of softening something rigid within. What blessing did you receive from that experience?

Rejoicing in God's Gifts

Give each person (who desires) an opportunity to share a simple tangible or intangible gift of God received this day.

Returning to God's World with Prayerful Hearts

- Spend a few minutes in silence in your closing circle and give each person (who desires) an opportunity to share something that he or she looks at through a lens of scarcity but would like to see differently.

- Go around the circle and pray (by name) for the person on your left, praying specifically for God to help your neighbor see the named thing through the lens of abundance.

Remaining Connected

- Hold in your heart the person on your left and pray daily for his or her desire to see differently.

～ Remember to reflect on scripture and pray daily for one another.

～ Read chapter 6 before the next session.

Session 6
SEEING WITH OUR SOULS

RECONNECTING WITH ONE ANOTHER

Reflect on these questions:

～ When did you most feel the presence of God this week?

～ When did you least feel the presence of God this week?

CENTERING THROUGH SILENCE AND PRAYER

Begin this part with a centering symbol if you chose one.

REFLECTING AND SHARING

Discuss chapter 6.

～ Reflect on an experience that you perceived as negative that turned out to be a means of growth. You may want to share your thoughts (but no names).

～ Think about a group or a person whom it is hard for you to call sister or brother. Try to get to the deepest reason. You may want to share your thoughts.

~ Discuss the story about Abba Poemen. Do you have a tendency to put the "right rules" above compassion? Is being "right" the same as being faithful?

~ Do you know persons who are experiencing *han*? How could you individually, or your group, or your church be involved in the negation of negation?

~ Have you experienced feeling so much passion for a person (or people on one "side") that you could not feel compassion for another person (or people on the other "side")?

~ Reflect on interconnection—both the interconnection of the global family and the rippling influence of events. Share your insights.

~ Have you ever had an experience in which someone was for the moment a living icon, a window to God's love?

RETHINKING A FAMILIAR SCRIPTURE

When we consider compassion and seeing with our souls, the fifth beatitude comes to mind:

Blessed are the merciful, for they will receive mercy. (Matt. 5:7)

~ The Aramaic words translated "merciful" and "mercy" are *lamrahmane* and *rahme*, respectively. Both words stem from the ancient root that relates to womb and also to compassion, evoking an image of giving birth to mercy. They also relate to love and pity.

~ Two versions of the fifth beatitude, translated from Aramaic, are these:

Blessed are those who extend grace; they shall find their own prayers answered.

Blessed are those who shine from the deepest place in their bodies. Upon them shall be the rays of universal Love.[9]

1. Compare these three versions of the fifth beatitude. What are their similarities and differences?

2. What do they say to you about showing compassion in your own life?

3. What do they say to you about the relationship between living compassionately and living abundantly?

REJOICING IN GOD'S GIFTS

Give each person (who desires) an opportunity to share a simple tangible or intangible gift of God received this day.

RETURNING TO GOD'S WORLD WITH PRAYERFUL HEARTS

∾ Go around the circle and offer a word of blessing and compassion to the person on your right.

∾ Close with prayer.

REMAINING CONNECTED

∾ Remember to reflect on scripture and pray daily for one another.

∾ Read chapter 7 before the next session.

Session 7
STEPPING OUT ON SHIFTING SANDS

RECONNECTING WITH ONE ANOTHER

Reflect on these questions:
- When did you most feel the presence of God this week?
- When did you least feel the presence of God this week?

CENTERING THROUGH SILENCE AND PRAYER

Begin this part with a centering symbol if you chose one.

REFLECTING AND SHARING

Discuss chapter 7.
- Share examples of nihilism in American popular culture. What can individual Christians and churches do to counteract the effects of this influence on youth in our circle of care?
- Did you find yourself fitting fairly well into one of the four categories of "strategies of action"? If so, which one? Does one of those categories describe your congregation?
- In dealing with globalization, Friedman specifically mentions the dimensions of politics, culture, international security, financial markets, environment, and technology. Each country has all of these dimensions. Can you think of recent examples of interactions in any of these areas?
- Share your feelings and thoughts about the capacity of science. When faced with all this, in what ways do we tend to

shrink our perspective instead of broaden it, such as reading the book *Zoom* backward?

∾ What can we do individually in our own small way, as a group and as a congregation, to help develop wise and moral guideposts in this amazing new world?

RETHINKING A FAMILIAR SCRIPTURE

Let's reflect on the sixth beatitude in relation to stepping out on today's shifting sands:

Blessed are the pure in heart, for they will see God. (Matt. 5:8)

∾ Again we have the Aramaic word *layleyn* (discussed earlier in Session 4), which is translated "those" and relates to waiting by lamplight in the night with a sense of expectancy.

∾ The word translated "pure" is *dadkeyn* in Aramaic. It relates to consistency in love (or sympathy) and also to influence and abundance connected with "a fixed, electrifying purpose."[10]

∾ The word translated "heart" is *lebhon* in Aramaic. It refers to a center that radiates life, which could be compared to the sun's radiation of light and energy. Vitality, desire, and affection are part of life shining from that center, as well as courage and even audacity.

∾ The word translated "see" is *nehzun* in Aramaic and also relates to contemplation and inner vision. The old roots connote a flash of lightning; we identify with this image when we get a sudden insight, an "aha!" experience.

∾ The Aramaic *alaha* is "God." The roots "point to the force
and passionate movement of the cosmos through the soul of
every living thing."[11]

One version of the sixth beatitude, translated from Aramaic,
is this:

Blessed are those whose passion is electrified by deep, abiding purpose;
they shall regard the power that moves and shows itself in all things.[12]

1. *Pure* denotes consistency, clarity, cleanliness (uncluttered
   by distractions or irrelevancies, distilled of impurities). We
   could have a pure heart, but we lack passion and purpose. If
   so, how might we respond to God's world?
2. *Passion* (as it is used here) denotes strong feelings. We could
   have passion but lack purpose and a pure heart. If so, how
   might we respond to God's world?
3. It is possible to have purpose but lack passion and a pure
   heart. If this is true, how might we respond to God's world?
4. What would change in our lives if we began to respond to
   God and God's world with deep, abiding purpose connected
   to passion and a pure heart?

RETURNING TO GOD'S WORLD WITH PRAYERFUL HEARTS

Close with a special time together that involves everyone, celebrates God's grace, focuses on gratitude, and offers an opportunity
to experience abundance of life in a way that is appropriate and
meaningful for your group. Be creative and trust the Spirit!

Notes

CHAPTER 1: SEEKING THE SECRET

1. Thomas Merton, *New Seeds of Contemplation* (New York: New Directions Books, 1962), 296 (italics mine).

CHAPTER 2: LONGING FOR BELONGING

1. Elias Chacour with David Hazard, *Blood Brothers* (Grand Rapids, Mich.: Chosen Books, 1984), 36.
2. Ibid., 91.
3. Henri J. M. Nouwen, *Our Greatest Gift: A Meditation on Dying and Caring* (San Francisco: HarperSanFrancisco, 1994), 64.
4. William Ashworth, *The Left Hand of Eden: Meditations on Nature and Human Nature* (Corvallis, Ore.: Oregon State University Press, 1999), 63.
5. Ashworth, 64.
6. Nouwen, *Our Greatest Gift*, 24.

CHAPTER 3: YEARNING AND DISCERNING

1. *The Confessions of St. Augustine*, trans. J. G. Pilkington (New York: Horace Liveright, 1927), 229.
2. Parker J. Palmer, *Let Your Life Speak: Listening for the Voice of Vocation* (San Francisco: Jossey-Bass Inc., 2000), 2.
3. Joan D. Chittister, *The Psalms: Meditations for Every Day of the Year* (New York: Crossroad Publishing Company, 1996), 69.
4. Dennis Linn, Sheila Fabricant Linn, and Matthew Linn, *Sleeping with Bread: Holding What Gives You Life* (Mahweh, N.J.: Paulist Press, 1995), 1.
5. Marc Gunther, "God and Business," *Fortune*, 9 July 2001, 68.

6. Chittister, *The Psalms*, 15.
7. Merton, *New Seeds of Contemplation*, 297.

CHAPTER 4: HEALING OUR HEARTS

1. Brother Roger, *Peace of Heart in All Things: Meditations for Each Day of the Year* (London: Fount, 1996), 96.
2. T. S. Eliot, "East Coker" in *The Complete Poems and Plays 1909–1950* (San Diego: Harcourt Brace Jovanovich, Publishers, 1952), 127.
3. John Wesley, *The Works of John Wesley* (Grand Rapids, Mich.: Zondervan Publishing House, n.d.), 1:225.
4. Rueben P. Job, *A Wesleyan Spiritual Reader* (Nashville: Abingdon Press, 1997), 186.
5. Merton, *New Seeds of Contemplation*, 297.

CHAPTER 5: REVIEWING OUR WORLDVIEW

1. Henri J. M. Nouwen, *Our Greatest Gift*; Parker J. Palmer, *The Active Life: A Spirituality of Work, Creativity, and Caring* (San Francisco: Jossey-Bass Inc., 1999); Walter Brueggemann, "The Liturgy of Abundance, the Myth of Scarcity," *Christian Century*, 24–31 March 1999.
2. Brother Patrick of the Hermitage at Harmony Hill, quoted in "Friends of Silence," January 2001.
3. Viktor Frankl, *From Death-Camp to Existentialism*, trans. Ilse Lasch (Boston: Beacon Press, 1959), 65.
4. Nouwen, *Our Greatest Gift*, 17.
5. Walter Brueggemann, "The Liturgy of Abundance, the Myth of Scarcity," 344.
6. Ibid.
7. Ibid.

8. Gunther, "God and Business," 32.

9. Ibid., 80.

10. Henri J. M. Nouwen, *Bread for the Journey: Reflections for Every Day of the Year* (London: Darton, Longman and Todd, 1996), 145.

11. David Steindl-Rast, *A Listening Heart: The Spirituality of Sacred Sensuousness*, rev. ed. (New York: Crossroad Publishing Company, 1999), 27.

12. David Steindl-Rast, *Gratefulness, the Heart of Prayer: An Approach to Life in Fullness* (New York: Paulist Press, 1984), 12.

13. Steindl-Rast, *A Listening Heart*, 40.

CHAPTER 6: SEEING WITH OUR SOULS

1. Chittister, *The Psalms*, 26. Ps. 103 cited on p. 21.

2. Andrew Sung Park, *The Wounded Heart of God: The Asian Concept of Han and the Christian Doctrine of Sin* (Nashville: Abingdon Press, 1993), 15–20.

3. Steindl-Rast, *A Listening Heart*, 107–8.

4. Chacour, *Blood Brothers*, 127.

5. David Bohm, "Postmodern Science and a Postmodern World," *The Reenchantment of Science*, ed. David Ray Griffin (New York: State University of New York Press, 1988), 65. Quoted in Park, *The Wounded Heart of God*, 148.

6. David Bohm quoted in Rushworth M. Kidder, "Living Proof of the Strange Quantum Ways," third in a five-part *Monitor* series, *The Christian Science Monitor*, 15 June 1988, p. B4, quoted in Park, *The Wounded Heart of God*, 149.

7. Charles Birch and John B. Cobb Jr., *The Liberation of Life: From the Cell to the Community* (Cambridge: Cambridge University

Press, 1981), 88, quoted in Park, *The Wounded Heart of God*, 150.
8. John B. Cobb Jr. and David Ray Griffin, *Process Theology: An Introductory Exposition* (Philadelphia: Westminster, 1976), 154, quoted in Park, *The Wounded Heart of God*, 149.

CHAPTER 7: STEPPING OUT ON SHIFTING SANDS

1. Penny Long Marler and C. Kirk Hadaway, "Methodists on the Margins: Self-Authoring Religious Identity," in *Connectionalism: Ecclesiology, Mission, and Identity*, vol. 1, ed. Russell E. Richey, Dennis M. Campbell, and William B. Lawrence (Nashville: Abingdon Press, 1997), 291–311.
2. Thomas Hibbs, *Shows about Nothing: Nihilism in Popular Culture from The Exorcist to Seinfeld* (Dallas: Spence Publishing, 1999), quoted in Roberto Rivera, "The Children of Nietzsche," *Touchstone: A Journal of Mere Christianity*, September 2000, 15–16.
3. Rivera, "The Children of Nietzsche, " 14–15.
4. Marler and Hadaway, "Methodists on the Margins," 294–95. They build on the work of Anthony Giddens, *The Consequences of Modernity*, who found four typical adaptive reactions to this shift: pragmatic acceptance, cynical pessimism, idealism, and radical engagement (Stanford, Calif.: Stanford University Press, 1990), 134–37.
5. Job, *A Wesleyan Spiritual Reader*, 186.
6. Thomas L. Friedman, *The Lexus and the Olive Tree* (New York: Anchor Books, 2000), 23.
7. Ibid., 47.
8. Ibid., 31.
9. Merton, *New Seeds of Contemplation*, 295.

10. The interview was by Robert Schuller, summer 2000.
11. Most of the information in the seminar can be found in Richard W. Oliver, *The Coming Bio-tech Age: The Business of Bio-Materials* (New York: McGraw-Hill, 2000).
12. Chacour, *Blood Brothers*, 129.
13. Brother Roger, *Peace of Heart*, 150.
14. Nouwen, *Our Greatest Gift*, 16.

GUIDE FOR GROUPS

1. Neil Douglas-Klotz, *Prayers of the Cosmos: Meditations on the Aramaic Words of Jesus* (San Francisco: HarperSanFrancisco, 1994), 47.
2. Ibid., 65.
3. Ibid., 50.
4. Ibid., 57.
5. Ibid.
6. Ibid., 56.
7. Ibid., 54.
8. Ibid., 53.
9. Ibid., 59.
10. Ibid., 63.
11. Ibid.
12. Ibid., 62.

About the Author

Marilyn Brown Oden is the author of the award-winning novel *Crested Butte* and eight nonfiction books. A former counselor, Oden leads retreats on spirituality and life transitions and has traveled all over the world to be with Christians in their life situations. She also maintains an active schedule of lectures on the Christian spiritual life. Oden holds master's degrees in both counseling and creative writing and received the Distinguished Achievement Award from Dillard University in New Orleans. She is a United Methodist laywoman.